THE REFERENCE SHELF   VOLUME 42 NUMBER 6

WEST AFRICA TODAY

EDITED BY

NANCY L. HOEPLI

Senior Editor, Foreign Policy Association

THE H. W. WILSON COMPANY
NEW YORK   1971

THE REFERENCE SHELF

The books in this series contain reprints of articles, excerpts from books, and addresses on current issues and social trends in the United States and other countries. There are six separately bound numbers in each volume, all of which are generally published in the same calendar year. One number is a collection of recent speeches; each of the others is devoted to a single subject and gives background information and discussion from various points of view, concluding with a comprehensive bibliography. Books in the series may be purchased individually or on subscription.

WEST AFRICA TODAY

Copyright © 1971
By The H. W. Wilson Company

International Standard Book Number 0-8242-0414-X
Library of Congress Catalog Card Number 76-149384

PREFACE

In a few short years West Africa has been transformed from a colonial outpost of the British and French empires into a patchwork of politically independent nations. From 1957, when Ghana gained independence from Britain, to 1965, when the Union Jack was lowered over Bathurst, Gambia, thirteen new nations emerged. With the exception of Liberia, founded in 1847 as a colony of freed slaves from the United States, the West African nations share a common colonial heritage. They also share with other emerging nations a multitude of problems: disease, malnutrition, low productivity, a shortage of capital and of trained manpower.

The striking feature of the fourteen countries of West Africa, however, is not so much their similarities as their differences. They range, in size, from Gambia with a population of less than a half million to Nigeria with close to 63 million; in geography, from landlocked desert waste to fertile coastal plain; and in resources, from a single crop to a diversity of agricultural and mineral wealth. For a few countries, the growth and development potential is good to excellent; for others, it is almost nonexistent.

The economic problems facing the new nations have been compounded by political instability. For most West African countries the first ten years of independence were tumultuous ones. By 1965 most of the cast of leaders had changed, and in not one country was there an orderly transfer of political power from one party to another through the electoral process.

The new leaders of the late 1960s were for the most part military men. In two countries the military were the principal actors in dramas which could have far-reaching implications for Africa's future. The first drama was the civil war in Nigeria. Had Biafra's secession succeeded, it

3

would not only have destroyed Nigeria, but, in the eyes of many observers, it could also have led to a continental secessionist epidemic. The Biafrans' struggle ended in January 1970; then under the leadership of Major General Yakubu Gowon the slow process of reconciliation and reconstruction began.

The second drama, a peaceful one, took place in Ghana. In 1969, true to their word, the military leaders who had run the country since they ousted Dr. Kwame Nkrumah in 1966 returned power to civilian authorities. With the election of a new president in September 1970, Ghana completed the transition to full civilian rule. The government may not survive; nor is there any certainty that other military regimes will follow Ghana's example. But if the new democratic government does succeed, it could mark a turning point in Africa's political development.

The story of West Africa's first ten years of independence, the defeats as well as the triumphs, is told in the following pages by Africans, Americans, British, and French, by correspondents and scholars, students and leaders. It is an unfinished story, one whose tension, it is hoped, the following selections will convey.

The editor would like to thank the various authors, publishers, and organizations that have granted permission for the use of materials included in this book.

NANCY L. HOEPLI

December 1970

A NOTE TO THE READER

For earlier surveys of Africa in the Reference Shelf series the reader should consult *The New Nations of West Africa* (Volume 32, Number 2), edited by Robert Theobald and published in 1960; *South Africa* (Volume 34, Number 2), edited by Grant S. McClellan and published in 1962; *North Africa* (Volume 38, Number 5), edited by Ronald Steel and published in 1967; and *East Africa* (Volume 40, Number 2), edited by William P. Lineberry and published in 1968.

CONTENTS

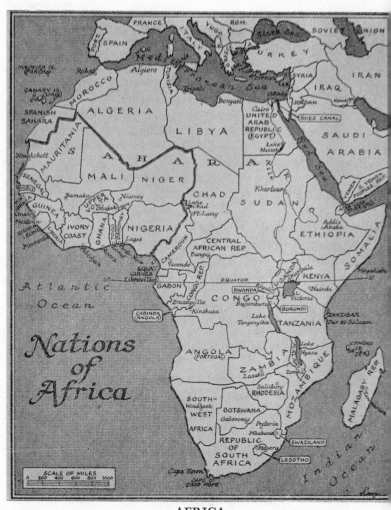

AFRICA
(West African states marked off by boldface line)

Map from *Current History*, March 1970, inside back cover. Reprinted by
permission of Current History, Inc.

THE INDEPENDENT WEST AFRICAN STATES

Country	Capital	Year of Independence	Pre-Independence Status	Population (UN mid-1968 estimate)
DAHOMEY	Porto Novo	1960	Part of French West Africa	2,570,000
GAMBIA	Bathurst	1965	British protectorate	350,000
GHANA	Accra	1957	Britain's Gold Coast colony and British Togoland	8,380,000
GUINEA	Conakry	1958	Part of French West Africa	3,800,000
IVORY COAST	Abidjan	1960	Part of French West Africa	4,100,000
LIBERIA	Monrovia	1847	Founded, with missionary assistance, by freed American slaves	
MALI	Bamako	1960	As French Sudan, part of French West Africa	1,130,000
				4,790,000
MAURITANIA	Nouakchott	1960	Part of French West Africa	1,120,000
NIGER	Niamey	1960	Part of French West Africa	3,810,000
NIGERIA	Lagos	1960	Former British colony and protectorate; joined at independence with UN Trust Territory of Northern Cameroons	62,650,000
SENEGAL	Dakar	1960	Part of French West Africa	3,690,000
SIERRA LEONE	Freetown	1961	British colony and protectorate	2,480,000
TOGO	Lomé	1960	French-administered UN Trust Territory	1,770,000
UPPER VOLTA	Ouagadougou	1960	Part of French West Africa	5,180,000

I. WEST AFRICA COMES OF AGE

EDITOR'S INTRODUCTION

For a majority of West African nations the year 1970 was a milestone. It marked the tenth anniversary of independence. How did the new states weather those first ten difficult and critical years? On balance, writes Dr. Ernest W. Lefever, Brookings Institution fellow, the former French and British colonies fared better than the pessimists had predicted in 1960 but fell short of the great expectations of the romantics.

A common obstacle confronting most West African nations has been the divisive pull of tribal loyalties and intertribal antagonisms. New York *Times* correspondent R. W. Apple, Jr., after having completed a nine-month swing through black Africa in 1969, reports on the conflict between allegiance to tribe and allegiance to nation.

In addition to tribalism there is, in the words of Washington *Post* correspondent Anthony Astrachan, a "host" of other "insolvables" which have severely tested the independent countries' ability to survive. The problems run the gamut from infertile soil and disease to untrained manpower and elitism. Some of the insolvables are described in the final selection.

NATION-BUILDING [1]

During the 1968 presidential campaign in the United States one of the world's largest land masses, embracing no fewer than forty sovereign states, went virtually unnoticed and unmentioned. . . . The candidates rarely spoke of Africa

[1] From "State-Building in Tropical Africa," by Ernest W. Lefever. *Orbis.* 12:984-90. Winter '69. Reprinted by permission. Dr. Lefever is senior foreign policy studies fellow, Brookings Institution; author of *Uncertain Mandate: Politics of the U.N. Congo Operation.*

or any African country. Neither produced a task force report on Africa. Africa did not even rate a footnote in the campaign.

This uncalculated nonchalance toward the ancestral home of one American out of every ten stands in sharp contrast to the expectant mood of Americans just a short decade ago when two dozen African colonies were on the brink of independence. The end of European control, an objective devoutly sought by the United States and the Soviet Union, each in its own way and for its own reasons, appeared to be in sight. In 1960 Washington and Moscow exaggerated the political significance of tropical Africa and entertained extravagant expectations in behalf of the newly emerging states, expectations not shared by the experienced African hands in Europe.

As the drama unfolded the highest hopes and worst fears of 1960 were confounded. The new states did not "go back to the bush," as the cynics predicted. Nor did they become peaceful democracies, as the romantics hoped. The record is mixed and the future uncertain. Independent black Africa has been torn and bloodied by tribal conflict and civil war in Nigeria, the Congo and the Sudan. There have been a score of coups, countercoups and abortive coups. Economic growth has been slow, and in some countries the economy has stagnated. On the positive side there have been no interstate wars, no tribal or regional group has succeeded in permanently fragmenting the territory of any state, and there has been slow, peaceful political development in a handful of countries, notably Kenya and the Ivory Coast.

Looking back, Robert A. K. Gardiner of Ghana, one of Africa's most respected statesmen, referred to the African drama as "a decade of discouragement." How could it have been otherwise? To an uncomfortable extent all peoples are prisoners of the past. The political resources essential to state-building in Africa are severely limited by the tribal culture of the precolonial era, the brevity and superficiality of Western influence, and the abrupt but peaceful transfer of authority from Europe to inexperienced political leaders. . . .

"A Female Continent"

The hundred million indigenous people living between the Tropic of Cancer and the Tropic of Capricorn belong to more than two thousand tribes and speak twice that many languages and dialects. The great majority of these people are illiterate and live in small villages. Their primary identity is the traditional tribe which circumscribes their social loyalties and their view of the larger world.

In a massive and precipitous shift of sovereignty, the political responsibility for these traditional tribesmen and their kinfolk who live in or near the European-built cities was transferred from mature governments in London, Paris and Brussels to fledgling African leaders. Partially Westernized and varying widely in education, political sophistication and patriotism, these politicians are determined to maintain and develop the thirty states bequeathed them by the European colonial powers.

The leaders of each new regime, large and small, have repeatedly declared their intention to develop a modern welfare state along broad Western lines, supported by an expanding economy based on foreign trade and investment, and secured by statewide military and police services. The fundamental political problem—the task of achieving a new order as secure as the colonial order and able to protect basic human rights and provide for a fuller life by means of increased productivity—will be grappled with for the foreseeable future within the framework of the existing territorial states. Though new legal entities—larger by reason of merging present states or smaller by reason of successful secessions —are possible, they are not likely in view of the tenacious opposition of the great majority of African leaders to any changes in the state boundaries drawn by the metropolitan powers.

To maintain and develop any new state is a formidable task. In black Africa this task has been exacerbated by the character of the precolonial culture, the ambiguous colonial heritage and the premature transfer of sovereignty.

Precolonial Africa south of the Sahara was largely an iron-age culture fragmented into a multiplicity of tribes and language groups. Unlike the Mediterranean world, black Africa developed no literature, no science, and only the most primitive forms of architecture and artifacts. The wheel and mathematical calculation were unknown. Animism was the dominant "religion." The primary social unit was the extended family, and the primary source of identity was the tribe which bound the imagination and historical memory of its members.

The tribe was also the primary political unit. The tribal chief wielded final political authority, though there were larger kingdoms established by the conquest of the stronger warrior tribes. Tribal wars were frequent and savage by modern Western standards. Ritual cannibalism and indigenous slavery were widespread. As Russell Warren Howe [in *Foreign Affairs*, April 1968] points out, Africa "created the Atlantic trade in slaves by stimulating a formerly disinterested market," and the "African leadership of the day fought fiercely against" the abolition of the slave traffic.

In terms of its physical and political environment, tropical Africa was passive. Howe describes it as a "female continent":

Black Africa . . . possessed no maps. With eighteen thousand miles of coast, it produced no oceangoing ships, no navies or navigators. It sent no trade missions or emissaries around the world, of which it knew—and contrived to know—nearly nothing. Indeed, before the pan-Africanizing experience of colonialism, each tribe was ignorant of almost all African lands except its own, and those of its neighbors and present or past enemies. A female continent, black Africa was to be "discovered," penetrated and dominated by others. There were few exceptions to this image of passivity.

This "secular inertia," says Howe, "helped make colonial domination inevitable."

The conquest of Africa by the European powers in the

nineteenth century had a unifying, not Balkanizing, effect upon the continent. It imposed upon over two thousand tribes a political system of some fifty administrative territories and six European language zones. The colonial administrators, along with Christian missionaries, brought education, medical care and better living standards. Law and order were imposed. Tribal fighting was greatly reduced, and the cruel excesses of the witch doctors and cannibalism were curbed. Slavery was virtually abolished. The rudiments of Western justice were made available to a large portion of the indigenous population.

Most consequential of all, the imperial presence in Africa created in the partially Westernized elite a sense of supra-tribal identity and a desire for political authority and autonomy coextensive with the territorial boundaries drawn by the Europeans, even though some of them cut across traditional tribal lines. But the colonial powers failed to prepare adequately either the elite or the larger population for wider political responsibility. Developing the desire for self-determination without creating the capacity for self-government was the ambiguous legacy of the colonial period.

Given these conditions, independence came too abruptly and too soon. The new states were established by fiat. Statehood was essentially a gift of the metropolitan power, based largely on an elite demand generated in part by the Western conscience and the desire of an increasing number of Africans to enjoy the material fruits of industrial society. The Africans did not win their independence by fighting for it. The fact that authority was handed over with little or no struggle and with almost no violence doubtless increased the severity of and delayed the reaction to the trauma of independence. It is axiomatic that men who gain political control over a territory by fighting for it against a determined foe learn more about the exacting requirements of exercising political power than men whose knowledge of politics is drawn largely from observing a colonial administration or participating in the civil service of an alien authority. . . .

From Colony to State—Tribe to Nation

When the political cohesion and coherence imposed upon Africa by European conquest was suddenly withdrawn without adequate provisions for maintaining order and security, the endemic centrifugal forces of tribe, language and region reasserted themselves. . . . Under optimal conditions the transition from colony to state can be effected quickly and smoothly, but even under the best of circumstances the transition from traditional tribal identity to a larger national identity is likely to be long and tortuous.

Decolonization in Africa can be described as the fragmentation of sovereignty at the periphery of empire. Under political pressures, large pieces of territory were cut loose, not to fend for themselves, but to become independent and self-determined states that would be sustained in large measure by continuing cultural, economic and security ties with the former colonial power. Seriously deficient in the disciplines, habits and institutions essential to modern economic and political development, these new states have been correctly described as weak, fledgling, embryonic, makeshift and soft.

A major reason for this weakness is that the transfer of legal authority is not matched by a transfer of power. The shift of sovereignty from London or Paris to a former colony, appropriately symbolized by a ceremony lowering an old flag and raising a new one, is a relatively simple transaction involving a commitment by the colonial power to cease exercising authority in the new state and a commitment by the new political leaders to accept the responsibilities of government. Political power and capacity, in contrast, cannot be transferred from one capital to another by a certificate of independence or by any other means. The capacity to govern must be drawn from the human and material resources of the new state. On independence day it is impossible to predict whether the newly installed government will develop that capacity, even though it has the assurance of help from the former metropolitan power or other friendly states.

It has been argued that most of the new African states are not economically and politically viable and that therefore their boundaries should be redrawn to create larger or smaller units corresponding to tribal or economic realities. This abstract argument flies in the face of the determination of the great majority of Africa's present leaders (with the notable exception of the Somalis) to maintain present state frontiers. On no other problem have they reached greater agreement than in their resistance to territorial changes by force or subversion. They show no disposition to merge their recently attained autonomy into more inclusive sovereign entities, or to create smaller units by secession. Even when it appeared that Biafra had a chance, only four of the forty members of the Organization of African Unity (OAU) recognized the secessionist state. As President Julius Nyerere of Tanzania said of the founding OAU conference in 1963, everyone present could agree that "our boundaries are so absurd that they must be regarded as sacrosanct."

A small state may be in a perpetually precarious position, but it is not an anachronism. . . . A small, poor and tribally diverse state with an overwhelmingly illiterate population can survive indefinitely if it is surrounded by benign neighbors and sustained by a propitious balance among the great powers. Under these conditions, plus trade, investment and other forms of support from industrial states, even a pocket-sized African state can survive and gain strength. Ultimately all weak states continue to exist with the sufferance of the more powerful states, whose interest in maintaining them may in some measure be induced by fear of hostile behavior on the part of other powerful states. The independence of the Congo in the 1960s, for example, was insured in part by the rivalry between the United States and the Soviet Union. Each sought to prevent the other from exercising control over this important country.

The persistence of tribal identity, thought, habits and social structures, in the great mass of tropical Africans, is the most serious barrier to national identity and the most serious internal obstacle to effective statewide government.

TRIBAL HERITAGE [2]

For the ordinary African, who lives in a hut in a bush clearing or on a parched savanna, "government" is still a remote abstraction.

His problems are the problems of life itself—food, shelter, birth, death. National balances of payments do not concern him, but he fears waterborne disease if he lives on the shores of Lake Victoria, drought in Senegal, man-eating lions in northeastern Kenya, coconut-palm blight in Togo.

In those circumstances the tug of traditional tribal loyalties is often irresistible. So the black man in the bush, like the white man on the American frontier one hundred years ago, seldom lifts his glance very far beyond his own horizon. . . .

The years since 1960 have been hard ones for black Africa, punctuated by coups d'etat, political assassinations (three in East Africa in 1969 alone), wars and rebellions. With only a few exceptions the regimes that brought the new nations into being have faltered or disappeared.

Separatist tensions underlie most African violence, and African political leaders have been unable to dampen them.

The most dramatic tribal split of the decade has, of course, been the one that has sundered Nigeria, the continent's most heavily populated—62 million in 1967—and potentially most powerful country. Since May 1967, it is estimated, more than a million members of the talented but assertive Ibo tribe have died from bombs, bullets or starvation rather than submit to union with the 300-odd other tribes of Nigeria. . . .

    [2] From "Tribalism Tears at Nations of Black Africa," by R. W. Apple, Jr., staff correspondent. New York *Times.* p 1+. N. 23, '69. © 1969 by The New York Times Company. Reprinted by permission.

Elsewhere in Nigeria tribal animosities run unchecked. A Hausa taxi driver in the northern city of Kano harangues his passengers about the "dishonest, uncivilized Yorubas" from Western Nigeria. The Efiks and the Ibibios in the vast delta of the Niger River insist that they can never again live under the same state government as the Ibos.

Animosities Unchecked

Even within a single tribe, the Yorubas, bitter regional differences have constituted a major factor in tax riots that have taken hundreds of lives....

In Ghana a national election goes smoothly, but the winning party, the Progress party of Dr. Kofi A. Busia, draws almost no support in the southeastern homeland of the Ewe tribe, a group as aggressive as the Ibos. All the Ewe votes go to the opposition National Alliance of Liberals—headed, not surprisingly, by an Ewe. . . .

Where tribalism is not a major factor, other forces promote disunity. . . .

The independent African states sprang to life within the boundaries drawn in the chancelleries of Europe late in the nineteenth century—boundaries that reflected the realities of imperial competition, not the realities of indigenous populations. With only minor modifications—Tanganyika and Zanzibar merged to form Tanzania, Italian and British Somaliland to form Somalia—the lines on the map have remained the same.

That means that Hausas live in Niger and Mali and Upper Volta as well as Nigeria, that Woloffs live in Gambia, Senegal and Mali, that Ewes live in Ghana and Togo, Yorubas in Nigeria and Dahomey. . . .

Nationalist pioneers in Africa such as Kwame Nkrumah of Ghana, who has lived in exile in Guinea since his ouster in 1966, thought that the answer lay in a United States of Africa. Ghana's first Constitution even provided for a surrender of sovereignty to a Pan-African union. But that ideal has faded rapidly as the governing groups in each new country tasted the psychic and economic fruits of statehood and sovereignty.

The Organization of African Unity is a pale relic of the great Pan-African dream, and its failure to end the Nigerian civil war has hurt its standing. In fact, the members of its Consultative Committee on Nigeria have demonstrated even more than most African leaders a determination to make the colonial boundaries stick.

Diallo Telli, the Guinean who is Secretary General of the organization, likes to quote the passage from its charter that enshrines "respect for the sovereignty and territorial integrity of each state and for its inalienable right to independent existence."

One remedy proposed for the problem of tribalism and separatism is a more even sharing of the spoils of office. The rebels in Chad, for example, are not likely to desist until some of their kinsmen move into positions of power in the government, the army and the civil service, and some of the corrupt southerners are dismissed from northern administrative posts.

"Our problem," said a Luo politician in Kenya recently, "is the same as lots of other tribes in Africa. We feel cut off from the government because we aren't permitted to participate in it very much. Why should a Luo look to Nairobi instead of the tribe?"

Reeducation Is Needed

But beyond that, it seems clear to students of African affairs, there must be a massive program of reeducation.

Dr. Thomas Lambo, a Nigerian psychiatrist who serves as vice chancellor (president) of the University of Ibadan, remarked several months ago that it might be a good idea to return to the old British colonial system of boarding schools, in which students from different tribes lived and studied together on a centrally located campus.

The system produced a large number of detribalized leaders—men like Judge V. C. R. A. C. Crabbe of Ghana—

but it has been almost completely abandoned, for reasons that are still unclear.

Zambia's thoughtful president, Kenneth D. Kaunda, believes that decades will be required to root out tribalism and that it will be accomplished only if the central governments "demonstrate that they can provide the sense of security and continuity that the tribe and the family can give."

Positive Side of Tribalism

Tribalism has its positive side, as Mr. Kaunda's remark suggests. It provides not only economic sustenance through the sharing of incomes but a sense of identity for the poor and the uneducated. Some anthropologists and others would be sorry to see it disappear.

But Africa is too far down the road of nationalism to turn back now, and it is impossible to build a modern nation and to strengthen it economically if there is no loyalty to the central authority.

The problems of tribalism and of economic and political development are intertwined. It is probable that tribalism and religious animosities will not disappear until there is something to replace the old verities. That something will have to be schools, hospitals, efficient and honest administration, and jobs.

Until the countryside is transformed—until economic development comes to mean something more than shining capital cities and European-owned businesses—further turmoil seems inevitable in black Africa.

UNSOLVED PROBLEMS [3]

In Africa, even more than in most places, you have to think like a pessimist and behave like an optimist.

You have to think like a pessimist because that is the only way to get an accurate estimate of the trajectory Africa

[3] From "Pessimistic Thinking May Make Africa Click," by Anthony Astrachan, staff correspondent. Washington *Post*. p B 3. Je. 1, '69. © The Washington Post. Reprinted by permission.

is following toward some intersection of natural disaster and social upheaval.

Once you have a realistic projection, it is possible to make sense out of behaving like an optimist. That may be the only way you can muster the energy to try to prevent Africa from arriving at that point between trouble and catastrophe. If the continent reaches target, the explosion could be merely firecracker revolutions—but it could also be blowups killing millions. . . .

Many African leaders have learned to be realistic in the sense that they no longer expect overnight economic development or political stability. Few, however, have learned how to combat, or even measure accurately, the poverty that surrounds their occasional trace of wealth. . . .

Criticism Is Resented

Africans seldom make . . . pessimistic appraisals of their situation. And like other people, they respond to gloomy analyses with a sense of insult. They feel that outsiders have little right to criticize their performance.

This lends irony to the fact that many of Africa's "accomplishments" are either refutations of racist predictions of quick disaster or corrections of Africa's own mistakes. Africa never degenerated into the chaos and race war that its enemies prophesied. Governments do function, even if many of them only maintain minimal law and order and collect minimal taxes. The corps of qualified civil servants is not large enough to do all the needed things well, a reflection on how little the colonial powers did to prepare Africans for developing societies, but that only makes the competence of the best African officials the more remarkable. . . .

More important than refutations of ignorant or prejudiced Cassandras is the ability Africa has sometimes shown to correct its mistakes. The stability the Congo has begun to show since the expulsion of white mercenaries in 1967 may not be entirely the result of political genius in President Joseph D. Mobutu, but it is a form of progress.

So is the reduction of subversion of some African states by exiles, noticed since Kwame Nkrumah was overthrown as President of Ghana in 1966. . . .

More affirmative accomplishments may yet fail to meet the goals Africa has set for itself, or through their very achievement create new problems beyond Africa's ability to solve. Take education, for example. In 1960-61, 36 out of every 100 children of primary school age in black Africa were in school. A UNESCO-sponsored conference of African education ministers put the target for 1965-66 at 47 per cent. In fact, only 44 per cent were in primary school when 1965-66 came around.

Kenya and Nigeria are more important examples. Both have expanded schooling beyond the economy's ability to absorb school-leavers (graduates and dropouts). In 1967, only 5 per cent of Kenya's 168,000 school-leavers found wage-paying jobs. In Nigeria, the number was nearly three times as high, the percentage probably less than twice as high.

Even if these countries' hopes for economic growth are fulfilled. which is extremely unlikely, they will be unable to give their educated or half-educated youngsters the kind of jobs they are demanding. Many of them already spout revolutionary rhetoric; by 1980 it may be revolutionary action. At least eight other African countries face a similar future.

A Host of Insolvables

School-leavers are one of a host of problems that seem beyond Africa's present ability to solve. These are reasons why many observers, including Africans and foreigners who love Africa and work hard to prevent catastrophe, think that the continent is heading for disaster, natural or social.

The list of insolvables begins with the natural problems —infertile soil, extremes of rainfall, debilitating diseases like malaria and bilharzia—that impoverish all but a handful of

African states. Solutions could be found—but only with money and technology that Africa does not have.

Next are the ancient social problems that Africa shares with most of the underdeveloped world and which hinder the effort to overcome the natural problems: low-yield farming methods; patterns of land use and ownership that make departures from subsistence farming often seem unprofitable; the extended family that deprives a successful individual of much of the reward of his enterprise.

Solutions to these problems require patience—in other parts of the world it took centuries—and radical imagination, a combination that is just as hard to find in Africa as anywhere else in the world, or more so. . . .

Another set of problems stemmed from colonial organization of African economies to provide raw materials for the homelands at prices set for the latter's benefit. Most African countries, like most developing countries everywhere, are still at the mercy of outside economic forces.

Their one-crop economies are profitable only with subsidies from the former metropoles. Fluctuating commodity prices sometimes lose producing countries more money than they get in foreign aid. Foreign supplies of capital and technology often mean foreign interference with a country's economy.

Another set of problems began with unfortunate styles that the colonialists saddled on Africa, but the Africans must share the blame for continuing them. One is the corruption. The meeting of traditional customs and modern methods transformed gift-giving into bribes; the idea of money as a key to success in societies that blurred Western distinctions between personal and communal wealth led to large-scale stealing that diverted resources from development in virtually every country in Africa.

An Educated Elite

A more serious problem in this set is elitism. Every country in Africa is torn by a rift between the educated and uneducated, the modern and traditional, the rich and poor, the urban and rural, the wage-earner and peasant. A recognizable elite — the educated-modern-rich-urban-wage-earners — controls the levers of power in every African state.

Development inevitably reaches a few members of society before the many, and the contrast may pit them against each other. But there was nothing inevitable about the way Africa made elitism a preferred ideology.

In a few states . . . there is a vote in which the masses can remove individuals from power, and do. In a few, there are signs that the elite sometimes listens to the people and keeps its policies within the few limits set by an inarticulate public opinion. Guinea and Cameroon each does this in a different way, though Westerners might have low opinions of their electoral systems.

In many African countries, however, the access of the people to the rulers, the best test of democracy outside the West, is closed off. Economic development and political power are tools used by the elite for their own benefit; the masses are lucky if they participate.

Even efforts to help the people can turn sour, as in the expansion of schooling that created the school-leaver problem already cited. At best, the governments thought the spread of education was the key to economic growth—but thought too little about what kind of education was needed or about the size of key that would fit their small growth possibilities.

At worst, the governments catered to the desire of the people for a diploma that they thought gave them membership in the elite. The elite did not notice how seldom the students actually acquired the education that the diploma symbolized, or how ready the people were to imitate the elite and snub the practical training that can give increased productivity and real economic growth.

Coup and Charisma

Two special kinds of elitism provide much of the news that Africa has made in the past three years and will make in the next few. One is the military takeover, in which one elite usually shoves another out of power. . . .

The second special kind of elitism is rule by an old man who incarnates his country's nationalism and enjoys the charisma that traditionally belonged to king, chief or elders in many African societies. He thinks his and his country's interests are synonymous and opposes almost all change, no matter how much of a revolutionary he once was. He resists change because it might interfere with his power.

Africa's prime examples are Emperor Haile Selassie II of Ethiopia and Presidents William V. S. Tubman of Liberia, Jomo Kenyatta of Kenya and Félix Houphouët-Boigny of the Ivory Coast. They have ruled their countries so long and so thoroughly that it is hard to imagine what will happen once they die—even if the probabilities favor some purely political process of change, as in Liberia and Kenya, rather than civilian upheaval (possible in the Ivory Coast) or military intervention (probable in Ethiopia).

A Skimped Continent

Some observers ask what makes Africa's disaster indications different from those of any other part of the underdeveloped world. One possible answer is that the rich nations have collectively done less for Africa than they have for Latin America and Asia in this century.

Another is that the synergism of Africa's problems may be greater than in any other part of the world: that is, their collective impact is greater than the sum of their individual impacts. Saddle a corrupt elite on a country using subsistence agricultural techniques on land that is semidesert except where it is flood plain or rain forest, and the result is worse than you would guess from any one of those problems.

Africa's problems are huge, and it has much less than it needs in skills and resources to deal with them. This often leads foreigners to prescribe grandmotherly advice, foreign aid tailored to the donor's needs more than to Africa's, or massive intervention. . . .

Intervention cannot help Africa if it comes in unacceptable forms. Africa can make it only by doing its own work and making its own mistakes. A friend may be entitled to note his observations of the way Africa is compounding the mistakes that nature and the colonialists committed there. He is not entitled to try to save Africa against its will.

Independent Africa has the right to go to hell in its own way. That is one of the things that independence means. If enough Africans think like pessimists but behave like optimists—or follow some other, better formula of their own devising—they may wind up at some more attractive destination. But you can't make them do it.

II. THE POLITICS OF INDEPENDENCE

EDITOR'S INTRODUCTION

West African governments in the sixties were racked by a succession of assassinations, coups d'etat and civil wars. Only four of the newly independent nations—Guinea, the Ivory Coast, Niger, and Senegal—survived the decade without at least one major political upheaval. In November 1970, President Sékou Touré of Guinea charged that an invasion force from the adjacent colony of Portuguese Guinea had attacked Conakry but was quickly repulsed. In December, after investigation, the United Nations Council voted to condemn Portugal.

In the opening selection, L. Gray Cowan analyzes the decline of the single-party system during the first five years. Military rule was the hallmark of West African politics in the latter half of the decade. Frederic Hunter, using tiny Dahomey as an example, explores the causes of coups. Four other military takeovers—those in Ghana, Upper Volta, Mali, and Togo—are described by Victor D. Du Bois, Francis G. Snyder, Pierre Biarnès, and William Borders. Their reports illustrate some of the differences and some of the similarities among West African military regimes.

The armed forces, for the most part, have shown little disposition to abdicate to civilian leadership. One exception is Ghana. Jim Hoagland and Frederic Hunter describe the orderly restoration of civilian government in this former Gold Coast colony. These articles are followed by a brief commentary from the London *Economist* on this change-over. And the section closes with two selections which assess the future of military rule in West Africa—one by William Gutteridge, the other by L. Gray Cowan.

THE POLITICAL PROCESS [1]

The pattern of postindependence African politics was characterized until 1965 by the presence of a single party or a one-party dominant system. . . .

The arguments of those in power in support of the single-party system were based on both pragmatic and theoretical grounds. The pragmatic justification was derived from the view that in the crisis following independence, a strong government was needed to weld the nation together. The needs and the goals of economic development were both imperative and evident; since there could be no argument regarding the goals, parties representing different points of view were considered superfluous. The single party, it was claimed, represented the will of the people. It permitted mass participation in decision making and since it did not represent the interests of a single group, a section, or an economic class in the population, it was, basically, the argument ran, more democratic than the Western multiparty system. The system of the single party was praised as a method of achieving national unification and of eliminating the tribal and local interests that stood in the way of genuine national solidarity. The single party was seen as the logical extension of the unification created during the period of the anticolonial struggle. It was not only the agent and the vehicle of modernization, but its presence as a unifying force was necessary if a viable society was to be maintained under the enormous stress of modernization.

Madeira Keita, an official of the Union Soudanaise, the governing party of Mali, stated the case clearly in an article published in 1960 in which he pointed out:

In the present historical situation in Africa there is no need to multiply parties, nor to indulge in the luxury of a sterile and fratricidal opposition. Since we were agreed on the essentials and

[1] From *The Dilemmas of African Independence*, by L. Gray Cowan, director of the Institute of African Studies, Columbia University. rev. ed. Walker. '68. p 5-18. Copyright © 1964, 1968 by Walker and Company, New York. By permission of the publisher.

were pursuing the same objectives, was there any reason to remain divided and split into parties that fought one another?

But Keita also recognized that the single-party system is not without its dangers.

But how to safeguard the ideals of liberty and democracy in the single party? . . . Democracy is the exercise of public authority in conformance with the will of the masses. . . . If there is one party it is necessary, first of all, that it be the true expression of the aspirations of the people. . . . This is only possible to the degree that the party is solidly organized and there is real discipline within the party so that decisions are taken only after lengthy debate and free discussion . . . ; the system of the unified party demands more honesty, more disinterest and more devotion from the leadership. . . . One can remain a leader in Africa for a long time only if one is really acting effectively.

In theory at least the single party was to be the point of aggregation of the whole spectrum of interest groups within the society, but in reality its larger function came to be a restructuring of society in line with the goals of modernization by eliminating those groups, such as the traditional leadership who stood in the way of modernization, and replacing them with new and modernizing interest groups, formed by the youths' and women's wings of the national political party.

The emphasis upon the single national political party was to have far-reaching consequences for the political structure of the new African states in the few years following independence. Almost by definition, the major agent of change was to be the national political institutions created by the party. As a result, the political process became of dominating interest, and the personality of the leader invested with an almost religious symbolism. Under these circumstances, the major functions of the party include not only rule making according to the vision of the new society espoused by the leader but also that of insuring that the rules of the new social structure are adhered to by the mass of the people.

The constitutional consequences of the single-party regimes were to personalize more and more power in the hands of a strong executive president with the simultaneous weakening of the representative organs of government left to the colonies by the European powers. Increasingly, legislatures became not forums for debate of public policy (it was argued that this was a luxury that only developed countries could afford) but merely formal ratifying bodies for decisions already taken by the party executive. In the absence of institutionalized opposition, parliamentary institutions became less and less meaningful as the government took over increasing areas of executive power. In theory at least, the executive president responded to popular pressures, which were to be exerted through the units of the mass political party since it represented the direct emanation of the popular will. In the absence of a traditional authority in the new nation-state, the party became the only effective means for the legitimization of power.

Foreign observers, and many Africans as well, argued that the single party was inevitable at this stage of African development. . . . The existence of an opposition party would not necessarily permit more freedom of discussion than did the single party because, according to the party theorists, there was opportunity for full freedom of discussion at every level of the party hierarchy below the leadership, and the foundation of party policy was to be the consensus deriving from this mass discussion of the important issues before the party.

Consensus Democracy

The concept of popular consensus derived, it was claimed, from the tradition of the African village meeting. It is true, of course, that most African tribal political systems provided methods for limited popular participation in political decision making. Few if any traditional rulers in Africa governed as autocrats; usually they were surrounded by councils of some type without whose consent no important decisions could be taken. In many instances, formal provisions were made for the expression of opinion concerning the replacement of a chief, or members of his council, who transgressed tribal mores seriously. It is equally true that these traditional provisions did not normally involve expressions of majority and minority opinion tabulated as individual votes. The strong inclination of African village politics toward consensus democracy is evident to anyone who has been present at such gatherings. The decision-making process in these meetings is based upon discussion, which because of its length and fullness gives everyone concerned a chance to express his opinion. The consensus finally reached is shared by all those present, thus obviating the necessity of a vote which would leave the community sharply split; it should also be added that under these circumstances, everyone also shares in the consequences of a decision, good and bad. Western parliamentary democracy with its roll calls and votes was not, many thought, suited to the African conception of communal decision. However valid this line of reasoning may be for African village government, it leaves out the critical point that it cannot be transferred to the process of decision making on a national scale any more than the democracy of the Greek city-state or the New England town meeting is suited to the process of present-day American national government. ...

The Decline of the Single-Party System

Beginning in 1965, the predominance of the single-party systems throughout Africa was seriously disturbed by a rash of military coups in which the leaders of the parties that had been in power since independence were either displaced from office, exiled, or in some cases even lost their lives. The political parties that they had built up over the past decade were banned, many of the leaders were imprisoned, and the powers of government assumed by a group of military officers who, for a temporary period at least, became the controllers of the destinies of their countries. In the light of the enthusiasm engendered by the political parties at independence, and the effort which followed to promote national unity through political organization and ideological

indoctrination, the sudden disappearance of these apparently strong parties has come as a surprise to the world outside
Africa. In nine countries—Nigeria, Ghana, Dahomey, Algeria, Congo (Kinshasa), Upper Volta, the Central African
Republic, Togo and Sierra Leone—the military assumed the
power directly, to popular acclaim. In several other countries, the threat of military force has been behind changes
in the regime . . . ; and in a variety of other countries, the
possibility or the rumor of a military coup has caused the
party in power to alter its policies in line with the demands
made by the military.

The direct explanation for a military coup must be
found for each country in the particular circumstances of
the country concerned, and each coup, therefore, deserves
individual study. However, a few generalizations might be
ventured regarding general factors that serve as a partial
explanation for all of this series of coups.

In part, the blame must be laid at the door of the political
parties themselves. In most countries the parties failed to
maintain the enthusiasm with which they were swept into
power at the time of independence. Moreover, after independence, they were unable to keep the promises of the
better life so rashly made during the anticolonial struggle.
The theory of the mass party with popular participation in
all phases of government was comparatively easy to maintain
in a period when the leadership could concentrate on the
single issue of independence and the major opponents were
the colonial administrations. There can be little doubt that
in most instances the leadership was prepared to continue,
insofar as possible, this high degree of mass participation
after independence. Indeed in such countries as Guinea, for
example, the early years of the regime were marked by weekly
meetings of the party at the village level, designed to involve
the whole of the adult population in discussion of the major
issues facing the government from day to day.

But with the development of governmental responsibility the attention of the leadership of the party everywhere

became distracted by a flood of new problems, both internal and external, requiring immediate decision. Shortage of trained personnel in the capital put extremely heavy pressure on the time of those who assumed ministerial posts, so that perforce they became less and less concerned with the explanation of party policy to the mass. No longer were they able to spend time traveling in the rural areas to defend party decisions in person. Moreover, the lines of communication within the party hierarchy were often seriously disturbed by the departure of trained local party leaders to take over posts in the national civil service at the capital. Local party leadership was thus forced back into untrained and inexperienced hands which, lacking guidance from above, were unable to maintain the degree of party discipline previously created with the *élan* of the independence struggle. To those in power at the top, the ideal of mass and open discussion appeared increasingly wasteful of the valuable time required for the day-to-day business of government, and in consequence there grew up a tendency to announce decisions of government affecting the lives of the people by fiat rather than through preparation by prior discussion. Correspondingly, less emphasis was given to the local party cells as sounding boards for public reaction, so that minor resentments which might have been avoided went unheeded. . . .

Repression and Reaction

It was inevitable, given the fundamental changes in society demanded by the broad goals of modernization enunciated by the party, requiring for their attainment the total mobilization of society, that the party's actions would create opposition. As cooperation failed and opposition grew, the ruling party tended to see in it not a rational critique of its plans but rather an opposition aimed at seizing power by revolution if necessary. The opponents of the regime came to be regarded as a threat, engendered by local or traditional interests, to the slender bonds of national unity which the party was seeking to strengthen. To meet this threat the leaders increasingly resorted to coercion when it became clear that persuasion was no longer successful. Because administrative and judicial power lay completely within its hands, the ruling party was able to pass restrictive legislation, such as the preventive detention acts, and to use the courts to enforce these measures. Where the courts proved obdurate or unwilling to deal with coercive measures, judges were dismissed and courts reformed. In a number of cases, as in Senegal, Mali, and the Ivory Coast, special political courts were established in which party officials sat as judges, to deal with offenses coming under the preventive detention and other similar acts. It is notable, however, that, even where the judicial process was perverted, the regime appeared to be unwilling to take the ultimate step of the death sentence, and many such sentences were later commuted to lengthy prison terms. From time to time, too, the leadership appeared to feel, as in Ghana, that repression had been too severe, and a number of those imprisoned under the preventive detention act were amnestied. But as coercion grew, so too did popular resentment against the regime, since for every political offender imprisoned, perhaps hundreds of his extended family and his tribe were alienated. Although it is true that the repression was aimed at individuals rather than large groups opposing the government, unlike the totalitarian regimes of Western Europe, nevertheless the sense of fear and insecurity engendered by the possibility of imminent arrest produced much more widespread disaffection, particularly in Ghana and in Western Nigeria, than the number of those persecuted by the regime would appear to justify. . . .

In the first five years of independence there is no case recorded in West African national politics where there has been a transfer of power from one party to another by the electoral process. Where opposition and therefore by implication the possibility of a change of governing party is not tolerated, the parliamentary system can no longer be meaningful. Where one party arrogates unto itself all powers, no constitutional structure of checks and balances, however elaborate, can prevent the autocratic use of that power. Until there is general agreement on the perimeters within which the political game may be played, no amount of tinkering with the representational structure will create a mechanism for the peaceful transfer of power. The experience of Europe and America seems to indicate that the creation of such a national consensus requires many decades or even centuries, and even when it is achieved there is no guarantee of its permanence. It is hardly to be expected that the new states of the African continent will have achieved this consensus within a decade and still less that, without it, an alien institution as complex as the parliamentary system will work. The single-party system is not unique to Africa, rather it appears to be a common phenomenon in the early years of national independence throughout the developing world. In itself it is not necessarily the creator of political instability, rather it is a manifestation of the need to control tensions created by the modernizing process. So far the African experience has proved that it is a long way from being the ideal instrument, but it is perhaps one that must be tried before more satisfactory instruments can be created.

MILITARY COUP IN DAHOMEY [2]

Waves wash from the Gulf of Guinea onto the old Slave Coast. Breezes rustle the oil palms of Cotonou.

There lies beneath them a lingering malaise.

Riots have broken out down the coast at Porto Novo, the Dahomeyan capital. In Cotonou, the country's largest city, workers and civil servants wonder if they will spread.

They also grumble over the government's austerity measures, including the recent 10 per cent wage reduction.

[2] From "A Decade of Unrest: What's the Cause of African Coups?" by Frederic Hunter, staff writer. *Christian Science Monitor.* p 9. Ap. 19, '69. Excerpted by permission from *The Christian Science Monitor.* © 1969 The Christian Science Publishing Society. All rights reserved.

There is plenty of evidence, it seems to them, to prove suspicions of government corruption. Nearby stands the symbol of the prime minister's rule, the $3.5 million presidential palace, which a poor country can ill afford. And now he is off in faraway Asia.

Although he lives well, the workers mutter, his government turns a deaf ear to labor demands and jails leaders who represent their views. At the same time the prime minister devises schemes to pack ministerial chairs with those who share his ethnic heritage.

So things appeared to Cotonou's discontented workers in late October 1963. It was a prerevolutionary situation.

Then the Porto Novo riots spread. Although the prime minister rushed back from Taiwan, he failed to restore order. After four days of demonstrations, the army yielded to popular pressure. It dismissed the national assembly and took control of the government.

Another African coup had taken place.

Since the beginning of this decade, the decade of African independence, there have been more than twenty coups in African nations. The next one may occur tomorrow.

Just where would be impossible to say.

But "why" can be answered with less difficulty.

Basically coups are manifestations of the instability which plagues all newly independent African nations. Each must cope with rapid social, political, and economic change; each is trying to catapult its population from traditionalism to modern ways of life.

The individual situations preceding the coups differ greatly, as do the incidents which trigger them. A study of the coups does suggest, however, that they share certain causative factors.

When the next coup comes it probably will result from a combination of these causes, all of them present in the 1963 Dahomeyan coup:

An ethnic factor

Economic chaos or its apparent threat

Political malfunctioning or imminent collapse

Anomic—or antisocial—behavior among the populace

Problems of social structuring

Military self-interest—enlightened or otherwise

Significantly lacking from the list is the ideological factor. Although it may appear to account for several coups—those occurring last year [1968] in Mali or Congo (Brazzaville), for instance—examination suggests that a combination of some or all the listed factors actually motivated them. . . .

In Dahomey, regionalism—with deep ethnic roots—contributed to instability. Postindependence politics there tended to deepen the ethnic identifications of the regional groups.

In Sierra Leone, young military officers took power after the March 1967 election gave conclusive power to neither of the two parties. The ethnic connection was tenuous, but served as a pretext. "We acted only to avert civil war," the officers announced. "This was an election clearly along tribal lines."

In other instances ethnic resentments have simmered over a long history. . . .

Economic problems harry most of Africa's newly independent nations. . . .

Dahomey, for instance, in 1963 faced economic stagnation. It was overdependent on palm oil and other agricultural products, saddled with a poor economic infrastructure, impoverished by a bureaucracy which ate up 70 per cent of the national budget in salaries, and forced to rely on French aid to an extent approximating clientage.

Complicating this situation were a surplus of unemployed "intellectuals" and labor organizations able to undermine the government in pushing their demands.

Active discontent of unemployed workers has toppled other governments. In . . . Upper Volta the army took control in January 1966, after riots against the imposition of austerity measures.

Time and again rioting citizens across the continent called upon the army to "do its duty" and take control of the government.

In Ghana, a drop in the world market price of cocoa, combined with heavy prestige spending and a tendency to make economic decisions on ideological grounds, drove the country to virtual bankruptcy. In the year before President Nkrumah's 1966 overthrow the cost of living jumped 30 to 40 per cent.

The failure of governments to function effectively—whether for structural reasons, inefficiency, or mismanagement—has led to widespread citizen distrust of political processes. The manner in which they have been altered—often without resistance—demonstrates their fragility.

According to some, the single-party state represented an attempt to develop an African governmental structure. In some respects it did approximate—more closely than parliamentary forms—certain indigenous political systems. And in theory, at least, the single-party state would facilitate channeling resources into national development, a high priority goal of most countries.

But at the same time that structure also served to stifle opposition effectively and to provide opportunities for graft. For these reasons efforts to install single-party governments often set off assassination or coup attempts, such as occurred in Ghana, the Congo Republic, and Sierra Leone. . . .

Conflicting social structures have increased the instability of many African nations. Ethnicity and incompatible traditional forms are aspects of this problem.

But gaps within the society are even more basic than these. The urban-rural gap, for instance: that separating the city-dwellers with their way of life and aspirations from the bush people, the country folk. There is the "elite-mass" gap between the educated elite and the bulk of the people which continues to live in largely traditional ways. Even within this elite a gap may exist between those who hold power and those who envision themselves in positions of power but are blocked from them by ethnic, educational, or other reasons.

Dahomey offers an excellent example of these gaps.

"Traditional people" comprise about 90 per cent of the population. Their way of life largely conforms to the established practices of their forefathers and their economy is one of subsistence.

The remaining 10 per cent belong to the elite, although only about 20 per cent of them—a mere 2 per cent of the population—have regular incomes. Because the "elitists" are educated, and westernized, they have different expectations than the traditional people.

More significantly, they see themselves as having different rights, as deserving of different treatment, opportunities, and incomes than the masses. To them the distribution system does not seem faulty when it accords elitists monthly incomes which significantly exceed the yearly incomes of traditional people. . . .

A recurring pattern in the African coups has been self-interested action on the part of the military.

In many cases officers have acted to preserve their own positions. In Mali, the Central African Republic and to some extent in Ghana and Dahomey, officers apparently feared that political militia might supersede them. Moving against the government eliminated that possibility.

In other cases, the officers disagreed with government policy and grew anxious about their national role due to budget cuts and other limiting measures.

Officers also have acted from loftier, more enlightened motives. They have taken power to curb debilitating corruption and drastic political malfunctioning or to restore order after a government's failure to do so.

In Dahomey, the interaction of these factors caused a malaise which Gulf of Guinea breezes could not dissipate. It produced four Dahomeyan coups in as many years. Other countries with a similar complex of problems have fared little better.

Unfortunately, military governments have failed to solve the problems of Dahomey. Civilians now are making yet another attempt to run the country, this time minimizing ethnic and regional divisions and squarely facing economic problems—or so they say....

In Sierra Leone's third coup, noncommissioned officers, provoked by professional grievances and the failures of the military regime, overthrew it and invited civilians to take control once more.

But the return to civilian government, though a recurring phenomenon, could hardly be labeled a continental trend. In other parts of Africa military governments are more firmly entrenched than ever. In some, like the Congo (Kinshasa), they have produced a measure of the political stability and economic resurgence upon which strong nationhood can be built.

If any trend can be discerned, it probably is that power remains with those who solve problems—or at least convince the people that they are trying. [Less than eight months after this article was written, Dahomey suffered another coup.—Ed.]

MILITARY RULE: GHANA AND UPPER VOLTA [3]

When the military first started to move into power in significant numbers, between 1964 and 1966, there was a general fear that an era of unrelenting repression and economic stagnation might result. Many Africans dreaded that a trend toward military takeovers might be established on their continent, bringing the harsh dictatorship that afflicts so much of Latin America.

Two assumptions were implicit in this view: first, that the civilian regimes displaced by the military had incarnated certain civic virtues which would now be sacrificed (parlia-

[3] From *Military Rule and Its Repercussions in West Africa*, by Victor D. Du Bois, an associate of the American Universities Field Staff. (West Africa series. v 12, no 6) '69. p 2-6, 11-13. Copyright © 1969 by American Universities Field Staff, Inc. Reprinted with permission of the publisher.

mentary or some type of "people's democracy," respect for civil liberties, a concern for the well-being of the masses, etc.) ; and, second, that the military establishment, with its innate conservatism, its obsessive commitment to law and order, and its lack of governmental experience, was incapable of assuming the burden of rule in such a way as to benefit the people as a whole.

The first assumption was unwarranted, for in most of the African states in which military seizures occurred these civic virtues simply had not prevailed. Under the harsh, one-man rule of President Kwame Nkrumah, Ghana could scarcely be characterized as a functioning democracy; nor could the Upper Volta under President Yaméogo. In both of these countries, the men who headed the regimes in power were notorious for their distaste for democracy. Their prisons were filled with men who had differed with them in politics. Civil liberties, as understood in the West, had much the same precarious existence in Dahomey, the Central African Republic, and Congo (Kinshasa) , other states in which the military took over from discredited civilian regimes.

Ironically, Ghana and the Upper Volta never enjoyed such liberty as they now [1969] have under military regimes. In both cases the military devoted themselves first to the maintenance of public order. Once this was secured, they set themselves to the more difficult task of rescuing the national finances from the disastrous condition in which civilian rulers had left them. In the Upper Volta this meant meeting a deficit of $16 million; in Ghana, it meant winning back the confidence of foreign investors in the nation's economy. At the same time, the new military rulers undertook necessary reforms within the government, ridding it of corrupt officials, abolishing archaic and inefficient practices, and coping with such problems as favoritism and nepotism. Yet despite these Herculean tasks, the military governments in both countries were able to grant unprecedented civic freedoms. For the first time since independence, political parties are now free to organize and campaign in both Ghana and the Upper Volta; newspapers are actually permitted to print uncensored criticisms of government programs and officials; and citizens are encouraged to participate in running their country's affairs as something more than mere sycophants.

In the Upper Volta and Ghana a large measure of freedom has been granted to labor unions not only to defend the interests of their members but—what has been unheard of in independent Africa—to strike! The new sense of freedom is evident in the schools and universities as well. Under President Nkrumah, neither the faculty nor students at the University of Ghana, one of the most prestigious schools on the continent, were at liberty to speak out publicly and without fear on national issues. The university campus was often the scene of parades by thugs of Nkrumah's all-powerful Convention People's party, held for the express purpose of intimidating members of the university community who might take a public stand against the president or his policies.

Similarly, in the Upper Volta both secondary and university students were often subjected to unusually stringent controls because of the suspicion with which they were regarded by the men in power. They were forbidden generally to hold meetings or conferences of any kind for fear that these would soon turn into forums of dissidence to the political regime. On those rare occasions when such meetings were allowed, invariably they were under the careful scrutiny of government security agents. The students, aware that they were being watched and their names taken down by these agents, would hew to the party line and carefully avoid expressing any views that might later be interpreted as antigovernmental and which, therefore, could be used against them.

In both countries, this situation has changed markedly. The University of Ghana has once again become what its founders had hoped it would be one day: a center of intellectual activity and free inquiry where neither the scholar nor the student is inhibited from publishing his findings or expressing his views on important issues of the day. In the Upper Volta, students are now free to hold congresses and give vent to their views without fear of being imprisoned. Within the context of their own society, the views expressed at many of these conferences, and the positions adopted by the participants, are fully as controversial and radical as those of comparable student groups in the United States, France, or Great Britain. Yet these are developments which have occurred under military regimes.

It is significant, moreover, to note that in both Ghana and the Upper Volta the military have shown every indication of keeping their promise to restore civilian rule once the internal social and financial situation of their countries has been nursed back to health. In Sierra Leone, which had been under military rule since April 1968, such a transition from military to civilian control has already taken place. If this trend continues, it will be a development of major significance for Africa. In general, while the military have not proved themselves in power to be as pure as they seem to view themselves, neither have they been as disruptive as civilians feared. Thus there is hope that the military, far from representing a reactionary and even regressive force on the African scene, may ultimately be the guarantor of a more genuinely free society.

Characteristics of the Military

In most African countries, as indeed in many non-African countries, the bulk of the men who make up the armies are conscripts possessing relatively little if any formal education. Literacy is not a requirement for induction into most African armies, just as it is not a requirement for voting or otherwise participating in the political activities of the nation.

In the former French territories, up to a few years ago when conscription programs were implemented by the African governments, many of the men who filled the ranks of Africa's meager armies were persons who formerly had served in the French armed forces. Many of these men not only had been stationed abroad (chiefly in France) but had also seen combat service in Indochina or Algeria.

As to the officers, many had been trained abroad. . . . France as far back as 1922 had established the Native Officer Candidate School at Fréjus. But the majority of young men admitted to this school came either from France's colonies in Indochina or the Near East. Moreover, the few who were enrolled from Africa had a markedly lower educational background than their comrades from other parts of the French Empire. Nevertheless, by 1960, the year that most of the French colonies in Africa were granted their independence, there were 170 officers of African or Malagasy origin serving in the French Army. There were also eight men studying at St. Cyr, France's major military academy. When the colonies acceded to independence, most of these men were repatriated to their countries of origin, at the request of their governments, and were entrusted with the task of forming and training the armies of the new states. . . .

How the Military See Themselves

That the military frequently turn out to be more effective administrators than their civilian predecessors is due in large measure to the fact that they have an exalted image of themselves which they feel obliged to live up to. Many military men feel that they are better equipped than civilians to rule their countries because, unlike the civilians, they are politically untainted. This supposed political purity emanates mainly from the fact that as military men they are usually not a part of any political party; indeed, in their professional capacity as soldiers they have remained almost totally aloof from the internecine struggle that characterizes politics. To many military men political parties are at worst a cancer which must be excised if the nation is to survive; at best they are a nuisance which must be tolerated but only so long as they abide by the strictures of good behavior as set down by the military themselves.

Military men who have seized power also presume that they are more pragmatic than their civilian predecessors. They are little interested in the purely ideological rationale of political action. Much more important to them are the practical results which flow from any policy decision—one reason why military regimes are so seldom popular with intellectuals. While the balancing of a budget which has been in chronic deficit may be a noteworthy achievement, it is not likely to be one which will fire men with the same ardor as a precipitate nationalization of a foreign-owned company or the vigorous denunciation of foreign imperialism.

The military, moreover, usually are convinced that they are less self-seeking than their civilian *confrères*. Whereas the latter, when they are in power, frequently indulge in all sorts of extravagances—sumptuous living quarters, high salaries, lavish receptions, frequent trips abroad, etc.—the military are the very personification of probity and austerity. In the Upper Volta, General [Sangoulé] Lamizana, although president of the republic, has eschewed the opulent living quarters of his predecessor, ex-President Maurice Yaméogo, in favor of the simple villa he occupied as army chief of staff. In Dahomey, General Christophe Soglo, during the brief period he was the head of state, did likewise. In both countries the lavish receptions which were commonplace during the previous civilian regimes virtually disappeared.

Finally, the African military realize that if the civilians in the country—especially the more recalcitrant elements such as the labor unions, civil servants, and students—refuse to acquiesce in their policies, the military alone are in a position to impose these by force of arms if need be.

For all of these reasons the military in Africa are convinced that their role in determining the political destiny of their countries is one of growing importance. It is now evident to them, as it is to many other elements in African society, that the institutions which nominally are charged with the task of maintaining order and assuring the normal functioning of society—the civilian governments and the mass parties—are often unable to do so. For the various reasons cited earlier, there is a societal breakdown, a void which is created and which only the military can fill. The military are convinced that they are the only group in society capable of keeping the whole political structure from collapsing, maintaining the cohesion of the body politic, and assuring the survival of the state as a nation.

MALI: YOUNG TURKS' REVOLT [4]

As recently as two years ago, few observers of the African political scene would have predicted a military coup in Mali. President Modibo Keita's stature at home and abroad, the organizational network of Mali's single party, the Union Soudanaise, the Africanization and relative honesty of the Malian bureaucracy, the apparent effectiveness of the party's ideological blend of history, Islam, and socialism—these assets seemingly outweighed the deficits on Mali's economic and political balance sheet. Yet on November 19, 1968, residents of Mali's capital of Bamako awoke to find their city cut off from the outside world by a handful of soldiers, the potential opposition disarmed, and the president of the republic soon to be arrested. Thus ended the first era of independent Mali's political history. . . .

Shortly after 1 A.M. on November 19, 1968, a group of young officers of the Malian army convoked their colleagues at the Kati military academy near Bamako and confronted them with their plan for a military takeover. Eight officers who opposed the scheme, including Chief of Staff Traoré, were arrested. A few hours later the Milice Populaire [People's Militia] was assembled, ostensibly to prepare a welcome for President Keita, who was returning from the annual economic conference at Mopti aboard the river boat General Soumaré. Their weapons were seized and their leaders arrested. With the Bamako airport closed and communica-

[4] From "An Era Ends in Mali" by Francis G. Snyder, a former Ford Foundation foreign area fellow. *Africa Report*. 14:16, 21-2. Mr./Ap. '69. Reprinted by permission from Africa Report Magazine.

tions shut down, a detachment of troops was sent to meet
Keita when his boat docked a few miles from Bamako.
Though he may have been warned during the night, the
president had no means of escape and was arrested, report-
edly after refusing to cooperate with the military to form a
new government. By midafternoon most former ministers
and CNDR [National Committee for the Defense of the
Revolution] members were in confinement. The government radio blared, "The hour of liberation has come. The
regime of Modibo Keita and his lackeys has fallen." Blood-
less except for brief clashes between the Milice and the army,
the coup had succeeded. . . .

Why the Coup?

Soon after the takeover, Foreign Minister Koné said in
Paris that the army had seized power to

end the radicalization of the Marxist regime. . . . After following
a policy of balance between the Marxist and moderate elements,
the former president decided in August 1967 to govern with the
backing of the toughest of the Marxists. The Marxist theoreticians
forgot Malian realities, having been more interested in political
agitation to mobilize the masses in their favor. The Milice Populaire and the Comités de Vigilance were created. The people were
bullied and harassed. . . . Now the team of young soldiers wishes
to clean up the country's economic and financial situation.

Indeed, the predominance in the provisional government of civilians and carryovers from the deposed regime
suggests that the coup was directed not so much against
Modibo Keita as against the vicious circle of inflation, ideological rigidity, and political tension that gripped Mali in
the last years of his rule. The former president, in his role
as moderator among contending pressure groups, was unable to hold the party and later the CNDR together. When
at last he allowed the "radicals" in the Union Soudanaise to
have their "active revolution" while the "moderates" carried out the rapprochement with France, he lost supporters
on both sides of the ideological divide.

But the young officers also had military reasons for intervening. Since independence the army had been a reluctant object of politicization (meaning neutralization) by the governing party. It had been dispersed throughout Mali and used to pacify and administer dissident Touareg tribesmen. According to a recent visitor to Bamako, army units were to have been sent to the Office du Niger in November to complete the harvest and do agricultural work. The Milice Populaire was to have taken over their camps, and it is even said that the army was eventually to be disbanded or put at forced labor. These irritants and rumors, most galling to proud young graduates of French military schools, were reinforced by factors that accentuated differences within the army and between the army and the party.

There was a generation gap between the younger officers and the senior group exemplified by Chief of Staff Sékou Traoré, a veteran of French colonial wars and the product of less sophisticated professional training than the recent graduates from France. Before Colonel Traoré took over the army in 1964 from his deceased predecessor, General Abdoulaye Soumaré, the government abolished the post of army chief of general staff and established the rank of lieutenant colonel as the highest grade allowable in the armed forces— a blow to military prestige. Traoré's cooptation into the CNDR in 1966 and his increasing identification by younger officers with the political old guard further diminished the chief of staff's authority, already weakened by differences in age and education. After the coup, the government announced that Traoré would be "permitted to retire" on May 1, 1969, along with four other lieutenant colonels and five majors.

Finally, after the onset of the "active revolution" in July 1967, the ominous activities of the Milice Populaire added to strains between the army and the party. The Milice, numbering perhaps 3,000 armed and undisciplined youths, was militarily no match for the French- and Soviet-trained army of 3,500. But as the "revolution" gained momentum, the

Milice set itself up as the guardian of revolutionary morals and arrogated to itself powers that seemed to threaten the army's position. Meanwhile it was getting what the army considered a disproportionate share of new weapons and new uniforms. After the coup, Foreign Minister Koné told foreign diplomats in Bamako that the deposed regime had encouraged these youths in "lies and slander, violence, and even murder" in an "immense political guerrilla operation with no immediate socialist objective." Humiliated and often insulted by Milice behavior, a group of young officers asked President Keita either to disband the Milice or place it under military control. Instead, President Keita allegedly planned to have a group of army officers arrested on November 25.

Long before they made their move, the junior officers seem to have favored preemptive action as the only means of protecting themselves and correcting an economic situation for which they held the "leftists" largely responsible. On the night of November 18, a sergeant who was not connected with the pro-action group and who knew that the government was preparing to move against the officers, saw one of the officers who was to be arrested. "What!" he exclaimed, "You're still on the loose?" The officer passed the word to his colleagues, who decided to act immediately.

SNAIL'S PACE RECOVERY [5]

Eighteen months after Modibo Keita was ousted as president of Mali by an army coup, the atmosphere in the capital is more relaxed. The Malians seem to be rid of their obsession about "spies," although special permission still has to be obtained to photograph the French-built bridge over the Niger. It is also apparent that individual liberties are better safeguarded than they were before.

[5] From "Mali After Keita's Fall: Snail's Pace Recovery," by Pierre Biarnès, *Le Monde* correspondent. *Le Monde* (Paris) Weekly Selection. p 3. Je. 3, '70. © 1970 by Le Monde Weekly Selection in English. Reprinted by permission.

The improved economic situation is reflected in the better stocked stores, at least in the capital; farm output, once flagging, has picked up considerably. . . .

The lifting of socialist restrictions in rural areas, and the liberalization of the trade in farm produce, especially grain, which took place immediately after the November 19, 1968, coup d'etat, undoubtedly contributed to the current economic recovery. . . .

But it is glaringly evident that Mali is in the throes of serious difficulties at the political level. There is deep uneasiness on the upper levels of society today where previously the regime did at least have the advantage of being enthusiastically backed by the senior civil servants and middle-echelon officials. With the collapse of the Keita regime, the governing classes have become frankly disillusioned and indifferent. This attitude is not helping the task of the new leaders who are running up against a kind of general apathy in their efforts to get the country going.

Deliberate Inaction

But the present Malian government does not appear to know exactly what it wants to do. It has refrained from making vitally important decisions in a number of areas. Observers get the impression that the government's reluctance to act is deliberate, intended to preserve unity at the top at any cost.

The officers who in November 1968 left their barracks to set up a National Liberation Committee (it is today Mali's highest political body) acted to restore a modicum of freedom and because they were tired of being knocked about. But they were hardly prepared to run the country, and had only the haziest notions of the difficulties, especially economic and fiscal, with which they were going to be confronted immediately. Faced with the harsh realities of a very trying succession, they do not seem to have acted in concert, and the divergences in their political ideas have become more marked as a result of rivalries between cliques and personal animosities.

The rise to the presidency of Moussa Traoré, a young lieutenant who played a decisive part in planning and carrying out the 1968 putsch, came as a shock to the officer corps, and many of its senior members did not accept the appointment without reservations. A large number of these officers were forced to retire and some were even imprisoned after the coup d'etat....

After they seized power, Mali's military leaders were forced to retain virtually all of the former regime's political and administrative personnel so as not to disrupt the public services. Quickly jumping to the conclusion that they were really indispensable, most of these senior civil servants became the zealous, and sometimes aggressive, defenders of the former regime's economic structures and policy trends of which they were the principal, if not the sole, beneficiaries.

At a national conference held in Bamako last summer at the initiative of the government and the thirteen-member National Liberation Committee, composed exclusively of military men, equally anxious to establish a dialogue with them, the civil servants did not hesitate to attack both groups. Since that time the military has taken pains to avoid a head-on clash with the civil service.

Despite promises made soon after the coup d'etat that constitutional government would be restored, nothing is being said about providing the country with new institutions approved by the people, and political parties are still banned. Only the trade unions are cautiously beginning to regroup. The trial of the principal leaders of the former regime appears to have been put off indefinitely.

This apathy on the part of the majority of the people, the political strains inside the group in power, and the underlying opposition of the old regime's cadres explain the difficulties the present government has in dealing with the serious economic problems which continue to embitter relations with France, whose financial assistance, in various forms is more necessary now than ever before.

TOGO UNDER MILITARY RULE [6]

Togo, a former French colony that has seen much more political unrest than so small a splinter of land would seem to deserve or justify, experienced another attempted coup d'etat a few weeks ago in which one man was killed and more than a dozen were arrested.

It is difficult to find anyone who regards the plot or the plotters as a serious threat. And that, in the opinion of many here, is a measure of this West African state's new stability.

In the three and a half years since power was seized by Lieutenant Colonel Etienne Eyadema, the tough young commander of the small army, a few tentative signs of well-being have begun appearing in a generally impoverished country.

A small but secure industrial base is developing, coffee and cocoa exports are increasing sharply and the government has balanced three annual budgets in succession without the French subsidies that used to come here and which still go to poorer former colonies such as Chad and Dahomey. . . .

Reputation for Austerity

President Eyadema, who has advanced himself to the rank of general, acquired a reputation for living modestly, without the flashy extravagances favored by some of the military men who run other African countries.

The president, who served with the French army in both Vietnam and Algeria, has admitted that he was the man who fired the shots that killed Togo's first president, Sylvanus Olympio, in a coup in 1963, three years after independence.

[6] From "Togo, After Years of Unrest, Exhibits Stability and Makes Gains on Poverty," by William Borders, New York *Times* correspondent. New York *Times*. p 12. O. 7, '70. © 1970 by The New York Times Company. Reprinted by permission.

At the time Nicholas Grunitzky, a former premier, became president, but four years later Colonel Eyadema announced that he and the army were taking over to "put an end to the confused political situation." He has been firmly in control since.

Under President Eyadema, who is still in his early thirties, a substantial road-paving program has begun, production of phosphate, the only significant mineral deposit, has increased by half, and the government has begun to deal with the substantial problems of education and health.

A problem it has notably not dealt with is vast Togolese smuggling, particularly across the Ghanaian border. Despite Ghana's displeasure, General Eyadema is not expected to do much about it since Togo benefits enormously from what is probably her major industry: She collects import duties on goods subsequently smuggled out and fees and export charges on goods smuggled in and subsequently exported legally. The levies add up to a substantial part of the $28.8 million national budget.

Millions of dollars worth of diamonds, cigarettes, whiskey and perfume are flooding in and out as traders take advantage of an unusually lenient import code coupled with strong demand in neighboring countries along the coast.

"They do not get these cigarettes in Ghana, so we take them over and they pay well," a bare-chested Togolese explained the other day as he and half a dozen friends filled a motor-equipped dugout canoe with Lucky Strikes.

His candor, and the fact that the boat was being loaded in the bright afternoon sun on a popular beach only a mile outside Lomé, reflects the lack of official concern.

Prices Quoted in Bulk

The countries on the losing end, principally Nigeria and Ghana, are not so complacent. Periodically, as in a parliamentary debate in Accra last week, they threaten to do something about it.

Togo and Ghana share a four-hundred-mile border that meanders through dense palm forests and over sparsely settled mountains. Like many borders in Africa, it was drawn by Europeans with little thought about tribes and natural boundaries.

"Obviously, smuggling in such areas is difficult to police," a Ghanaian guard conceded at his post at the frontier, which is just at the Lomé city limits.

A few blocks away, on the palm-lined main square, merchants quote their prices in bulk on goods packed for transport through the bush or across the broad, blue Bight of Benin: $30 a case for Johnnie Walker Scotch that would cost $100 in New York, $108 for 50 cartons of Pall Mall cigarettes that sell for $4.35 a carton.

Another factor contributing to the situation is that the Togolese have declined to grant the preferences that most of the other former French colonies in Africa give to goods from France, so that American and Far Eastern products are competitive on the smugglers' market. . . .

The goods smuggled into Togo and exported legally consist largely of cocoa and mineral products from Ghana.

Togo, a land half the size of New York State whose population of about two million is about that of Queens [a borough of New York City], is part of what used to be the German colony of Togoland, and there is still a German aspect to the place, from the remnants of Gothic architecture to the superior domestic beer.

After World War I, administration of the territory fell to Britain and France, and the British sector subsequently became part of Ghana.

The rest became Togo, a land so narrow along its serene, sandy coast that one of its formidable market women, dressed in bright red and blue and carrying, say, a load of palm fronds on her head, could easily walk from one border to the other in a couple of days.

Earlier this year that trek was in fact being made by thousands of aliens expelled from Ghana who flooded across

the western border to stay in Togo or go on to Niger, Dahomey and Nigeria.

Most Are Subsistence Farmers

The Ghanaians, who acted in the face of great unemployment and a hard-pressed economy, have published no
precise statistics on the number forced to leave. In Lomé it
is thought that at least 30,000 Togolese came back. Some
officials were apprehensive about the effect on a country
where there are only 27,000 people holding salaried jobs,
nearly half of them in the government.

Africa's traditional extended family system, in which the
door is never closed to a relative, seems to have taken care
of most of the refugees, although unemployment continues
to be high.

The principal Togolese occupation, across the coastal
forests and in the lush northern highlands, is subsistence
farming.

The plantation system, which has exploited the poor in
other countries, has never taken hold in Togo, and the main
cash crops, cocoa and coffee, are usually grown on small
family farms.

Togo's free-trade policies, while doing so much for the
smuggling business, give some sharp competition to the few
industries that she has, and some critics of the government
say that it is being shortsighted. Unrestricted imports of
cottons from Japan, for example, have hampered the cotton
industry—something that other governments might have
chosen to protect with high tariffs.

Nonetheless, according to impartial observers, General
Eyadema's popularity is increasing and there is less talk
these days of either a change of government or a return to
completely civilian rule.

After the unsuccessful coup last month a series of popular
demonstrations took place around the country in support
of the president. Such demonstrations here are almost never

spontaneous, but there are indications that this time, at least, some of the people really meant it.

GHANA: THE MILITARY BOW OUT [7]

"So the military is leaving and the civilians are coming back. A year from now, we'll be sitting around talking about the good old free and easy days under the soldiers."

One of Ghana's top editors smiled wryly as he spoke of his nation's recent elections and the targeted September 30 [1969] return to civilian rule after 3½ years of military-police government. His comments reflect some of the paradoxes created by this precedent-setting event for Africa.

The 1960s, which began as the decade of independence for Africa, is ending as the decade of armed takeovers. Military coups have swept across this vast continent, and coup leaders occupy the seats of power from Algeria to the Congo.

The military has invariably coupled its seizures with guarantees of individual rights and promises to return power to democratically chosen civilians just as soon as the soldiers have straightened out the mess.

The promises have been hollow—except Ghana. Here the military regime allowed a remarkable outpouring of free speech. And now the soldiers are returning to the barracks. This turnover is being carefully watched throughout Africa for its possible implications.

Two Factors

Many persons here, Ghanaian and resident foreigners, suggest that the narrow aim of the 1966 coup, and the nature of Ghana itself, are the key factors in the turnabout.

The first point is discussed in Major General A. K. Ocran's recently published *A Myth Is Broken*. A careful reading of this slender book elicits the conclusion that

[7] From "Ghana's Army Gladly Hands Over Reins to the People," by Jim Hoagland of the Washington *Post* Foreign Service. Washington *Post*. p A 20. S. 23, '69. © The Washington Post. Reprinted by permission.

Ghana's army took power primarily to protect itself, and not to transform society.

Ocran helped execute the February 24, 1966, coup that sent Kwame Nkrumah into exile in Guinea. Ocran also has been a top member of the six-man National Liberation Council that replaced Nkrumah.

His book catalogs Nkrumah's squandering on grandiose projects that left no money for equipping the army. Ocran emphasizes Nkrumah's undercutting of career officers, and his habit of replacing them with junior officers more loyal to him.

Personal Army

Nkrumah seems to have sealed his own fate with a half-completed plan to raise and command personally "The President's Own Regiment," a Soviet-trained force that would have equaled the largely British-trained regular army. This, Ocran says, was a plot to "gradually . . . strangle the regular army to death."

The spur for the coup, then, was the army's own insecurity, and not the corruption that riddled Nkrumah's administration, nor the jailing of 2,000 persons for political waywardness (although these factors played a role in the takeover and accounted for its popular support).

Having shown a muscle it can flex again, the army feels secure enough to give the civilians another chance, observes one source close to the National Liberation Council. And the military gained more security in the August 29 election.

K. A. Busia, who was overwhelmingly elected prime minister, had the open support of the military council's chairman, Brigadier General A. A. Afrifa. Politically Busia is heavily in debt to Afrifa.

In any event, Busia will have to work under a three-man presidential commission that has limited veto powers. The commission, added to the constitution just before the elections, is made up of Afrifa, Ocran and the national police commander, J. W. K. Harlley.

Second Rationale

A noncontradictory but less Machiavellian rationale for the return to civilian rule is given by many who see Ghana as Africa's most politically sophisticated nation.

"This goes back to our heritage," said one intellectual. "The military knew we would not stand for their staying around one minute longer than seemed necessary."

Tradition has always kept the political pot boiling here. Chiefs were never autocrats, but ruled through the consensus of a council of elders. If the people found that chiefs acted unwisely or arbitrarily, they deposed them—often to the discomfort of the British colonialists who came to Ghana and tried to rule through local figures.

The British eventually attempted to lay a foundation for successful parliamentary democracy here. Ghana in 1957 became the first black African nation to be freed from European colonialism.

And, for all his disastrous domestic policies, Nkrumah put Ghana in the world spotlight with his aggressive Pan-Africanism and stirring speeches about independence. Ghanaians are aware and proud of the symbolic political value their country has always had.

Free Speech

"The soldiers would have been faced with an open revolt if they had not lived up to their promises," the intellectual continued. "It is that simple. They have done a good job, but now it is time to go."

The soldiers have generally won the admiration of their countrymen. Following Nkrumah's near police state, the council permitted an ebullient outburst of free speech. . . .

An influential businessman said:

The trouble now is that we are all so enamored with free speech that the new government is going to find itself faced with anarchy while we all run around spouting off about everything.

The new government will not be as secure as the military was [he continued]. It probably won't be able to permit itself the luxury of as much free press, at least for a while.

THE CIVILIANS RETURN [8]

Ghana has a democratic government again.

Good to their pledge, military and police leaders of the National Liberation Council, which rescued this West African nation from the misrule of Kwame Nkrumah, have brought about the orderly restoration of civilian rule. . . .

The restoration of the country has not been easy so far. Rivalries within the military, for instance, twice jolted the National Liberation Council (NLC). In April 1967, the first and more serious incident took the form of an abortive coup by two lieutenants. During it General Emmanuel Kotoka, the chief leader of the coup against Nkrumah, was assassinated.

Later, corruption threatened to compromise the NLC's credibility. In April . . . [1969] it was discovered that Lieutenant General Joseph Ankrah, head of the Council, had received payments, said to be political contributions, from a number of foreign firms. Disgraced, the general was forced to resign. He was replaced by Brigadier A. A. Afrifa, who now heads Ghana's three-man Presidential Commission.

The NLC has also met some resistance in one of its major areas of effort, economic reform.

In order to rescue Ghana from bankruptcy, the military and police leaders rescheduled the country's debt load which at the time of Nkrumah's ouster amounted to nearly $450 million in five years' debits alone. They transferred some state corporations to the private sector. They closed others altogether, those which were unprofitable or served largely to give an aura of economic prestige.

As a result large numbers of workers found themselves both without jobs and, due to the stagnation necessary to restore economic stability, without employment prospects.

In the other sector of major effort, the political area, the NLC initiated reforms with few adverse consequences. First,

[8] From "After Nkrumah: Ghana Puts the Pieces Together Again," by Frederic Hunter, staff correspondent. *Christian Science Monitor.* p 9. S. 20, '69. Excerpted by permission from *The Christian Science Monitor.* © 1969 The Christian Science Publishing Society. All rights reserved.

it banned the Convention People's party and its various wings. It placed their leaders under protective custody.

Reforms Initiated

Then, in a more positive vein, it undertook to effect reforms necessary for an orderly return to civilian rule. It established a Center for Civil Education under the direction of Dr. Kofi A. Busia, an Oxford-trained sociologist now chosen as the country's new prime minister. With branches throughout the country the center sought to teach the people at large about the workings of government and about their responsibilities as Ghanaians in the democratic processes which would eventually replace NLC rule.

It also set up an eighteen-member commission to draft a new constitution and an Electoral Commission to register voters, conduct orderly and free elections, and chart the path toward the transfer of powers to a civilian government chosen by the people.

A man instrumental in the work of both these commissions is Justice V. C. R. A. C. Crabbe. A true founding father of Ghana's Second Republic, Justice Crabbe has acted as both the Interim Electoral Commissioner and the Legal Draftsman of the new constitution.

"Every constitution reflects a country's experience of the immediate past," says Justice Crabbe. "That of Ghana's Second Republic is no exception.

"We were quite aware of Nkrumah's manipulations of the law," the High Court Justice continues. "I myself was drafting legislation and knew exactly what was going on."

The new constitution combines parliamentary and executive systems of government. While the majority party leader acts as prime minister and head of government, the constitution vests the roles of head of state and commander in chief in the Ghanaian president, a person over forty years who is, according to Justice Crabbe, "expected to be above politics."

Although he is not truly an executive, the president has to attend to more than purely ceremonial functions. He appoints certain key officials—the Auditor General, the Ombudsman who has investigative powers, members of commissions and corporate directors of the government-owned information media—and these officials are directly responsible to him. In addition he has certain powers to delay legislation.

"The most important addition to this constitution," says Justice Crabbe, "are the provisions regarding human rights, twenty-three pages of them. The most significant is the provision that any person fearing infringement of these rights—for anyone, not just for himself—can have recourse to the courts."

As further protection of these rights, the role of the judiciary has been enhanced and numerous obstacles—too numerous, say some observers—have been placed in the way of amending the constitution.

Dignity Is Evident

Discussing the elections with this reporter in his plush office atop the Electoral Commission building, Justice Crabbe speaks animatedly. He laughs frequently and strokes his white-fringed beard. Beneath the laughter and animation resides a dignity which somehow does not tally with the reports of his occasional tours of the farthest reaches of Ghana wearing a white vest with the words *Vote early* printed upon it.

Justice Crabbe declares himself satisfied with the conduct of the August 29 voting.

"Yes, I think the calm during the elections signifies the political maturity of the people," he says. "People are making too much of tribal divisions in the results," he continues. "Tribalism is not as deep seated in Ghana as elsewhere in Africa."

He answers an insistent telephone. "What's going on up there anyway?" he asks the caller.

He is inquiring about a polling station in the north, one of some 8,000, where balloting has been delayed because of floods. Electoral officials have had to be flown in by army helicopters and some mixup has occurred.

"Well, let's get it taken care of," he says, hanging up.

Turning to his visitor he explains: "The voters are trying to hitch rides on the helicopter." He laughs again and brushes his moustache.

Yes, he admits, there have been charges of election irregularities. "But if the people making these charges want them investigated," he adds, "they should file petitions with the Electoral Commission and stop talking so much to the press." He smiles again mischievously.

The work of the Electoral Commission will continue, he explains. For example. it must conduct an entirely new registration of voters, using photographic equipment this time. He himself, however, will return to the courts. He pats a stack of files.

"I already have four decisions to render," he says.

Overwhelming Mandate

If returning Ghana to civilian government has not been easy, the process of strengthening democratic rule and assuring its survival may prove even more difficult.

Dr. Busia's government has received an overwhelming mandate from the people. His Progress Party holds 105 out of 140 National Assembly seats, exactly 75 per cent.

Now Dr. Busia and his colleagues must tackle the myriad problems besetting this nation. They must try to lighten Ghana's debt load so that debt servicing does not continue to stifle the economy. They must alleviate unemployment. They must rescue Ghana's vital cocoa industry, said to be in a worse state now than ever before.

They must stem the flight of youth from the land. They must demonstrate to Ghanaians that the government intends to treat all regions and all tribes equally. They must seek to ensure the existence of a strong and viable opposition so necessary to the democratic process.

They must further the country's development, not only politically, but in terms of housing, road construction and repair, and in terms of better use of Ghana's human and material resources.

That makes a long list of imperatives. But it poses the questions:

Can democracy solve Ghana's problems? Can democracy survive those problems?

Many observers doubt that it can.

Others are more hopeful. In February 1966, they point out, the National Liberation Council's list of imperatives was no less lengthy, no less overwhelming. The skepticism about military leaders voluntarily relinquishing power was no less profound. But that relinquishment has come too.

It is an impressive act of self-denial and dedication to democratic ideals. Ghana's military leaders have taken the first hard pioneer steps toward guaranteeing the establishment of democratic rule in their nation.

If the civilian leaders follow their footsteps, they will set a precedent—and possibly an example—for all of Africa.

GHANA ONE YEAR LATER [9]

It doesn't happen very often, and when it does it deserves to be recorded. The election on Monday of Mr. Edward Akufo-Addo as Ghana's new president marks the final departure of the army from the government of that country. A national liberation council composed of soldiers and policemen ruled Ghana from the overthrow of Dr. Nkrumah in 1966 until October of last year [1969]. Then power was returned to civilian hands with the election of Dr. Kofi Busia as prime minister.

But the vestiges of military rule were still embodied in a three-man presidential commission, headed by Brigadier Akwasi [Amankwa] Afrifa. Mr. Akufo-Addo, a former chief justice, now takes on the responsibilities of this commission.

[9] Article entitled "Ghana: One of the Few." *Economist* (London). 236:30. S. 5, '70. Reprinted by permission.

The transition to civilian rule is therefore complete, and Ghana joins Dahomey in the distinction of being the only countries in Africa where the army has voluntarily and completely relinquished power after taking it over. The men who toppled Kwame Nkrumah in 1966 have proved their commitment to democratic principles. There are plenty of countries in Africa—not to mention Greece and others outside it —where that commitment remains to be tested.

The dissolution of the presidential commission came early in its maximum life of three years, and much earlier than many people expected. The reason, Brigadier Afrifa explained, was to put across the lesson that "people in power should not try to perpetuate themselves as if it were their property." The power in question is not enormously great, as Mr. Akufo-Addo will find. He will be much less than an executive president, though more than a purely ceremonial one. He will not exercise the very extensive power of his predecessor, Dr. Nkrumah, and in particular the power to remove supreme court judges. Of this he has good cause to be glad, having himself had experience of its abuse.

MILITARY RULE ASSESSED [10]

The period 1966-70, may be categorized as that in which the national armies of Africa began finally to emerge from the colonial chrysalis. . . . There is no doubt now that over large parts of tropical Africa the military have become a political force, not only because of what they have actually done, but because of the knowledge of what they might do in the future. In Ghana, for instance, where a peaceful transfer back to civilian rule has been executed, the possibility of a fresh intervention by the armed forces remains a factor in the political situation.

The experience of the last seven or so years in Africa, and the perspective of the last four, make possible an assessment

[10] From introduction by William Gutteridge to *The Armed Forces of African States, 1970* by Richard Booth. (Adelphi Papers no 67) Institute for Strategic Studies. 18 Adam St. London WC2N 6AL. '70. p 4-5. Reprinted by permission. Mr. Gutteridge is the author of numerous books, articles, and contributions to symposia about Africa.

of the role of the military in politics and their contribution to stability or instability. The qualities and capabilities, which enable armies to intervene politically, are now well recognized. Even the smallest armies have carried out successful coups, though naturally their ability subsequently to administer is inhibited by the number of trained men available. Neither the Ghana nor the Nigerian governments, after the 1966 coups, were thoroughgoing military regimes, but relied heavily on civil servants in their former roles. Arms, communications equipment, transport, and, in particular, basic administrative skills, along with the necessary cohesion and facilities for conspiracy, have been shown to be the essential qualities. . . .

The high success rate of attempted military coups seems to be attributable to their popular acceptability rather than to the outstanding political sensitivity and efficiency of their organizers. Colonial defense forces were generally regarded with fear as agents of imperial repression, and yet within a few years their heirs often appeared as saviors. It is a puzzle how, in new African states, the armed forces came so readily to be seen as patriotic by definition and possessed of unusual virtue and rectitude. But the period since 1966 has been one in which military regimes have done something to disperse their initially favorable image. The Juxon-Smith administration in Sierra Leone, for instance, failed to live up to the general reputation of military regimes for cleaning up corruption. This is only one illustration of what may be a general truth, that familiarity with military regimes tarnishes the image, because it is essentially impossible for them to honor it. Except possibly in Ghana, military rule has so far proved an inappropriate basis for political reorientation. The armies of Africa have proved no exception to the general rule, that they are not appropriate channels for political change. They are useful for the purposes of suspending political activities in a deteriorating situation, and having done so may prove capable of administering, but not of governing. The evolution of policy and new bases for legitimacy has generally eluded the politically involved African armies over the last four years. The foreseeable future will certainly provide more examples of military coups in Africa, and in particular, recurrent interventions where they have already occurred. . . . In general, the indications are that, while there are bound to be local explosions, it will require the injection of a major new factor radically to change the African military scene over the next two or three years.

THE FUTURE OF MILITARY RULE [11]

The duration of military rule before the return of power to civilian hands can only be estimated in most general terms. . . . By training or by inclination, the military officers are not in any country expert wielders of the type of political power that requires manipulation of the masses and decisions based on the delicate compromise of interests of widely varying groups. Once established in a position of political control, however, the military may be increasingly difficult to dislodge the longer they stay in power.

It should be pointed out in this connection, however, that there is no necessary implication that the military is anywhere committed to the creation of a two-party or multi-party system. None of the military leaders came to power on the basis of a promise to eliminate the one-party system. It would be naïve to expect that because the more conservative attitudes of the military indicate a somewhat more pro-Western stance than has been displayed by the politicians of several of these countries hitherto, any greater effort will be made to replicate Western parliamentary institutions in any overall sense. Moreover, no matter what the form of government may be when it is given over to civilian hands, the threat of the return of the military must be constantly in the minds of the next generation of politicians. Once

[11] From *The Dilemmas of African Independence*, by L. Gray Cowan, director of the Institute of African Studies, Columbia University. rev. ed. Walker. '68. p 22-4. Copyright © 1964, 1968 by Walker and Company, New York. By permission of the publisher.

having proved that it is possible to seize political power in response to the shortcomings of civilian government, the military will not soon forget that the process can be repeated.

The fact remains, moreover, that the military regimes in themselves can do little to change the fundamental problems of development faced by most of the countries in which they are now in power. Admittedly, a greater degree of efficiency and honesty may be achieved by the elimination of the former civilian masters. The basic difficulties, however, of countries such as Upper Volta and Dahomey derive not so much from the failure of the previous governments to create the necessary conditions for economic development but rather from the absence of natural resources which would permit a level of economic activity sufficient to meet popular demands for higher standards of living and a full degree of employment in the modernizing sector. No regimes, civilian or military, can satisfactorily solve this dilemma under present conditions since the capital needs for development are so great as to be beyond immediate prospect of attainment either from domestic savings or external aid. The military is, of course, only too well aware of this, and it may well be that the knowledge itself will hasten the return to civilian rule since the military will inevitably wish to avoid damage to their professional pride and position by seeing the stigma of failure laid upon them. On the other hand, if the military can establish for a reasonable period of time conditions of internal political stability, they may well be able to encourage external private capital investment to a degree that the civilian governments were unable to do.

III. NIGERIA: SECESSION AND SURVIVAL

EDITOR'S INTRODUCTION

As the most populous nation in Africa and potentially one of the richest, Nigeria deserves separate consideration. When the federal state of Nigeria gained independence from Britain in 1960, the eyes of Africa and of the world were upon it. If parliamentary democracy succeeded in Nigeria, it could have a profound effect on other new nations. If it failed, the consequences for Nigeria—and for Africa—could be disastrous.

In the opening selection, Professor David J. Murray looks at the stresses and strains in Nigeria's postindependence political system which led, first, to a military takeover and, finally, to civil war. Next, an African, Primila Lewis, discusses the harmful role of tribalism in Nigeria in the 1960s. Biafra's secession is then looked at from both the Biafran and the federal side in the first-hand reports by Renata Adler and Stanley Meisler. Following this, the role the foreign powers played in the war is analyzed by Walter Schwarz.

The concluding selections include two articles from *Newsweek* on the end of Biafra, the second presenting an Ibo view, an article by veteran correspondent Colin Legum reviewing the problems of reconstruction as Nigeria enters its second decade, and a *Newsweek* article evaluating Nigeria's progress toward nationhood.

POSTINDEPENDENCE POLITICS [1]

With the surrender of Biafran forces on January 12, 1970, thirty months of bitter fighting came to an end. The world's

[1] From "Nigeria After Biafra," by David J. Murray, professor of government, The Open University, Buckinghamshire, England. *Current History*. 58: 135-8+. Mr. '70. Reprinted by permission of Current History, Inc.

attention had been focused on Biafra's battle for survival in the face of a Nigerian army determined to obliterate it as an independent state. Yet there was more of interest in the recent history of Nigeria than what had been for Nigerians a civil war between the federal government and a relatively small group in the society.

For Nigerians, the central issue was the attempt to refashion the whole order of government and society to overcome the major problems of the past (of which the civil war was only one facet). To many Nigerians, the first Nigerian republic, which lasted from independence in October 1960 to the first army coup in January 1966, suffered three overriding limitations. First, the constitutional order produced an inflexible political system. The departing British had saddled Nigeria with a federal constitution, which included three constituent regions; of these the Northern Region contained more than half the population of the country. These regions were large and powerful entities—the smallest was larger than all but six independent countries on the African continent—and they had an existence as independent governments that predated the federal government. Party politics was based on the regions. The prime focus of attention was control over the regional machinery of government, and control over the federal government was based on interregional alliances. With only three regions (four after 1963, when the Mid-West Region was carved out of the Western Region) and with the Northern Region containing more than one half the country's population, there was little room for maneuver at the federal level. The federal government was almost inevitably controlled by an alliance of the agents of the Northern Region with another region; until 1965, the ally was the Eastern Region.

What made this inflexibility in the political system at the federal level more serious was the character of regional politics. In each of the Northern and Eastern Regions, a single party had gained control of the regional government and each ran its region on the basis of a single-party authoritarian regime. In the Northern Region, the Northern Peoples' Congress (NPC) was a party of the aristocracy from the emirates and (having had power transferred to it by the departing British) used the machinery of the regional government to impose a control to which it would brook no challenge. In the Eastern Region, the National Conference of Nigerian Citizens (NCNC) was a mass party of the Ibo-speaking majority. The party gained control over the regional government on the basis of majority electoral support and, as far as the Ibo-speaking population was concerned, it operated a relatively open political system. But for the 40 per cent of the population who were not Ibos, regional government appeared to be a system for allocating all benefits to the Ibos and using the machinery of government—regional and local government, courts and police—to repress opposition and criticism among minority peoples.

Two other circumstances exacerbated the general political situation. First, neither the Northern aristocracy nor the Eastern Ibos were satisfied with their alliance at the federal level, and each saw the other as committed to finding a way of excluding the other or establishing a firmer grip over the federal government. Second, this uneasiness was heightened by the political situation in the Western Region. There, particularly after 1962, because no party had a dominant influence, the state of politics allowed the Northern and Eastern regional governments to intervene in the hope of establishing a dependent ally who could be used to gain a predominant influence in the federal government. By 1964-1965, the NPC government of the North and the NCNC government of the East were financing and furthering what amounted to a near civil war in the Western Region in their attempt to establish an ally in control of the regional government.

The third and final limitation of the first republic was the general lack of probity, honesty and public spiritedness in government at all levels. Government was perceived as an instrument for the personal advantage of individuals and their clients; there was a high degree of defalcation and dishonesty and little concern for the public interest.

Well before Nigerian independence, disquiet over the constitutional order and the conduct of government had been expressed, particularly among groups known as the minorities—those, paradoxically, who formed a non-Hausa majority in the population of the country as a whole—Fulani in the Northern Region, non-Ibo in the Eastern Region and non-Yoruba in the former Western Region. Military coups created the opportunity for change. The first army coup in January 1966 was followed by an attempt to sweep away the federal structure and replace it with a unitary state. However well-intentioned, these measures were widely interpreted as Ibo schemes to gain undisputed control over the whole country, to achieve through army action what the Ibos had failed to achieve by other means. The innovations were planned and carried out by the coterie of fellow Ibos with whom the Ibo supreme commander surrounded himself.

The Second Coup

The second army coup of July 1966 replaced this tightly knit group of Ibos with a collection of military officers, civil servants and nonofficials, many of whom were drawn from the minority peoples. Thus Yakubu Gowon, the supreme commander, was an Angiva from the middle belt of Northern Nigeria, the head of the civil service was a Bini from Mid-Western Nigeria, and the Federal Executive Council contained leading opponents of the ruling parties in the former Northern and Eastern Regions. These individuals were not involved in the old rivalry between the Ibos and the Northern aristocracy and they were unsympathetic to the past constitutional and political order which had allowed affairs to be conducted at the federal level and in the regions for the benefit of two restricted groups. Unlike their immediate predecessors, however, they did not see the establishment of a unitary state as the solution to Nigeria's problems. Disparities in educational, economic and social

development in different areas, the size of the country, existing loyalties, and the distrust of centralized rule all militated
against a unitary state. Instead, in March 1967, the federal
government announced the abolition of the existing regions
and their replacement by a new federal structure in which
the constituent units were twelve states.

The twelve-state structure was designed to overcome two
of the three basic weaknesses in the first republic. It removed
the problems that arose from having only three constituent
regions, with one containing more than half the population
of the country. With twelve states there was more opportunity for flexibility in the political system of the country.

The twelve-state structure also overcame, at least in its
existing form, the problems of single-party authoritarian
rule that had arisen in the Northern and Eastern Regions.
During the period of military rule, party activities had
been banned, but even with the return of political activity,
the established parties would no longer be able to rely on
the machinery of the regional governments. Conditions had
been created in which parties would have to compete once
more for support, instead of using coercive authority.

Beyond these two objectives, the twelve-state structure
was also designed to increase the strength of the federal
government and thus to increase the degree of attachment
to Nigeria. None of the state governments had the power or
authority of the former regional governments, and even
without a redistribution of legislative powers and financial
resources, the federal government was more powerful than
it had been in the first Nigerian republic. Attention could
be expected to shift to the federal government simply because the largest concentration of distributable resources
would be found there.

Unfortunately, the federal government failed to gain the
support of the Ibo-speaking people of Eastern Nigeria for
its plans for a new constitutional structure. To those in
power in the Eastern Region, the decree of May 1967 creating the twelve states was a device for removing from their

control land, oil under that land, and thus wealth. The creation of the East-Central, South-Eastern and Rivers States out of the former Eastern Region became the immediate cause of the attempted secession of Eastern Nigeria and the creation of Biafra.

Biafra announced her independence on May 30, 1967. For the next thirty months, the future of the Ibo-speaking people was one of the major issues in world politics, as a devastating civil war swept the region.

AN AFRICAN VIEWS THE WAR [2]

As the Swiss-based Biafran campaign wins an increasing number of hearts and minds, it also increases the terrible hatred, bitterness and mistrust that must be overcome before any solution is possible. This hatred, which is purely tribal, is in turn making inroads into other African states with similar problems. "Another Biafra" is a warning cry going up in more than one country. This is a dangerous situation indeed. But certain facts must be kept in mind. The first is that the federal principle is crucial to Africa. However, the federal principle cannot succeed anywhere unless it is based on a clearly defined ideology which cuts across tribe, personal ambition and class distinction. These are the factors which plague current-day Africa and unless they are overcome bitter strife is inevitable.

In Nigeria, the federal system has been devoid of both a real national policy and a guiding social ideology ever since its inception in 1953. It is this which has led to its present impasse.

The great need is for both sides to overcome the vitiating factors of the past and forge a leadership of "new" Nigerians. The great hope is that young Nigerians, imbued with a new vision, will take a hand in the affairs of their country with

[2] From "Tribalism Must Die . . . An African Verdict," by Primila Lewis, writer for the *Daily Nation* (Nairobi, Kenya). *Atlas.* 16:46-7. D. '68. Reprinted by permission from *Atlas* Magazine (December 1968). From *Daily Nation*, Nairobi.

the same spirit which has moved the young intellectuals of Germany, the United States, France, Czechoslovakia, and even South Africa, to question and protest the validity and the purpose of their respective social systems.

Tribalism

For the truth is that Nigeria's political history right up to the present day has been a solidly tribal-oriented one. This is a fact which both federal and Biafran propaganda tend to evade.

When Colonel Odumegwu Ojukwu [leader of the Biafran secession] claims (as he did in his speech at Addis Ababa) that "it was the Biafrans who had dedicated themselves to the proposition of an internally coherent and unified state," he is overlooking the fact that at no point in Nigeria's history as a federal state has there been a genuine, nationally based party.

Independence was seized without a single party being able to win an overall majority in parliament. Hasty compromises were reached between regional parties with widely differing programs and platforms, and vital problems were left unsolved. . . .

All along then, Nigerian politics had been marked by an absence of any ideology other than that of personal and tribal ambition. Corruption was rife, and mismanagement, nepotism and bribery were rampant.

It was this state of affairs which led to the army coup of January 15, 1966. The coup was led by a group of junior officers, four of whom were Ibos, and one a Yoruba. Their leader was a dedicated and progressive young Ibo, Chukwuma Nzeogwu.

For the first time a group of people were totally committed to all the people of Nigeria. Unfortunately, due to behind-the-scenes meddling (some say by Ojukwu himself), the coup backfired. It was conspicuous that while the leaders of the North and the West were eliminated, the Ibo leaders on the death list escaped.

In the resulting confusion, General [Johnson T U Aguiyi-] Ironsi took control. Ironsi was a reactionary figure who took advantage of the initial popularity of the coup to install himself, arrest his rebellious junior officers, and then consolidate his position on an openly tribal basis.

Time for Decision

The golden chance was lost, and Nigeria slipped back into the cynical indifference of old times. What followed is well known. However, to my mind, this war has laid open one of the fundamental decisions which confronts Africa. As one political scientist has pointed out, this is Nigeria's time of self-determination.

For the first time Nigerians must decide for themselves whether they want one Nigeria, and why they want it so. Those Nigerians who have consciously identified themselves with the federal cause have not done so lightly. They have been forced to reexamine their assumptions and their attitudes. They have been made to remove their tribal blinkers and recognize clearly the significance of what they are fighting for. *This war means that tribalism must be abolished.* It has to be, if Africa is to succeed.

An African Verdict

For every time a "Biafra" happens, Africa loses a little more of her freedom—a little more of her right to freedom. Each "Biafra" means another foothold for a foreign power (in this case, France—only if Biafra succeeds, of course). Every "Biafra" means a notch up for South Africa's racist regime. A carved-up, wretchedly weak, "free" Africa is exactly what South Africa and all neocolonialists want.

The Nigerian intelligentsia must—as I think many of them do—understand and accept the significance of what they are fighting for. They are not fighting out of obstinacy or to "teach the Ibos a lesson." They are fighting for freedom.

The argument that you can't force unity at the point of a gun is a true one. But I must state here I do not accept the Biafran propaganda about federal intentions of genocide.

Nor do I accept that Britain, Russia and the UAR [United Arab Republic] are fiendishly contributing toward this end. I do believe that the Biafran propaganda machine has run away with itself, and that the Ibo masses have been tragically misled.

What Nigeria needs is a complete overhaul of leadership. It is the old-time professional politicians who have betrayed Nigeria. Their leadership is bankrupt and out of date. They are the sacred cows of Nigeria, and unless they are discarded a new Nigeria cannot be forged. It is essential that the new leadership give Nigeria a firm ideological base which cuts across tribes. And an honest social policy, the sole concern of which must be the *equal advancement of all Nigerians.*

LETTER FROM BIAFRA [3]

It is almost impossible to fly into Biafra now, or out of it. The relief organizations (Caritas, World Council of Churches, Nord Church Aid, Canadian Air Relief) that still fly to Biafra from the Portuguese island of São Tomé have formed a single operation, Joint Church Aid, which flies about five planes a night, sometimes two flights per plane, sometimes three, depending on the availability of pilots and the condition of planes. Always at night. . . .

The sense here is of a people about to die in isolation and pretending not to know it—convinced in any case by their recent history that they have no choice. Victims are seldom pure, or even entirely attractive, and a case can certainly be made against any victim of murder before some higher court of absolute irrelevance. But Biafrans (fighting a war, in a sense, for a position argued in Hannah Arendt's *Eichmann in Jerusalem [A Report on the Banality of Evil]*

[3] Reprinted by permission from article by Renata Adler, free-lance writer and critic. *New Yorker.* 45:47-8+. O. 4, '69. © 1969 The New Yorker Magazine, Inc.

are determined to avoid at least the accusation of passive complicity in their own destruction and resist, trusting their own interpretation of what the risks of capitulation and the costs of survival might be. Once the foremost advocates of Nigerian unity, they have been persuaded by a series, both before and since the war, of broken accords, systematic exclusions, and outright massacres, both total and selective (including the killing of all males over ten years old in a captured Biafran town where civilians did not leave), that Nigeria intends to eliminate the peoples of the region that is now Biafra, and that the intention of genocide is not one that you test, passively, until the last returns are in. In the massacres of summer 1966 (nearly a full year before Biafra's secession from Nigeria), thirty thousand natives of the Biafran region were murdered. "I have just been reading *Exodus,*" Professor Nwosu told a group of friends, some time after his night of waiting at State House. "Before the war, a novel to me was a trivial thing. But I should have known the West would not be impressed by thirty thousand. Some of you literary people should have told me." In 1966, pressure to withdraw from Nigeria came mainly from the Ibo people (who make up the majority of the population of the Biafran region), and it was the Ibo intellectuals, spread out over Nigeria and the world, who wavered. Now the situation is different. The intellectuals have returned from their jobs in the outside world to Biafra, to extremity, and to a people with whom, in their own worldliness, they were not even entirely familiar. An Ibo civil servant, educated elsewhere in Nigeria, when he is asked the word in Ibo for a sash in which local women carry their babies on their backs, does not know, until it is pointed out to him, what you are talking about, and he certainly does not know the word. English has always been Biafra's intertribal language, but conversations even in Ibo are interspersed now with English expressions, and the Biafran fondness for euphemism has a British ring. The war is everywhere referred to as "the crisis," areas of Biafra destroyed or occupied by Nigerian forces are always called just "disrupted" or "disturbed." The elite are leading now, as perhaps in war they always do. But Ibo society is, by tradition, individualistic and ruled by tribal consensus. The leaders and their ministries are unprotected to a degree uncommon in a country at war. If the people did not support their leaders, they could, being armed almost to a man, overthrow them. Biafrans now prefer the bush to the risks of Nigerian occupation, and Nigerian troops entering Biafran towns now find them empty. What defections there are, like that of Dr. Nnamdi Azikiwe, an Ibo who was once President of federal Nigeria and who recently turned from the Biafran to the Nigerian side, preoccupy Biafrans continually—perhaps because there have been so few of them. A betrayal in 1967, by Brigadier Victor Banjo, who had been put in charge of all Biafran forces in the Mid-Western Region, recurs in war-inspired songs all over Biafra. (Dr. Azikiwe's case is complicated by the fact that he had spent several months in London, in a state that his physicians described as "delayed shell shock," before going to Lagos and, when his extensive Nigerian properties had been returned to him, denouncing Biafra.) The favorable reaction in the American press to Dr. Azikiwe's claim that Biafran fears of extinction are a "fairy tale" presumably gave the Nigerians confidence to resume, a few days after the first editorials, their civilian air raids, bombing and strafing an orphanage at Ojoto. Dead: one nurse and fourteen children, miles from the nearest battle zone.

The former Eastern Region of Nigeria, which since May 30, 1967, has called itself Biafra, has always been the most densely populated region in all of Africa—and, in recent times, the most highly developed and educated black country there is. Its present population is about ten million; present size, ten thousand square miles; war dead in two years, one and a half million civilians by air raids and starvation, half a million more soldiers and civilians killed in actual combat zones. There are several hundred thousand refugees in Biafran refugee camps, millions more living with distant relatives in the traditional Ibo stress claim of the "extended family," seven or even twenty persons to a room. Biafran roads, before the bombings the best roads in Nigeria, are pitted now, interrupted by checkpoints and occasional rows of tree stumps to impede enemy landings, eroded further by the intense rains, sometimes hollowed under the tarmac to stop heavy armored vehicles, but crowded in the late and early hours of darkness by defiling lines of people—trekking, with burdens on their heads, to relatives, to markets, to shelter or hospitals. Kwashiorkor, the ugly, mortal protein-deficiency disease, which had almost been stopped when Red Cross flights were running at strength, is afflicting children again, and the people on the roads include a high proportion of adults damaged, bandaged, or in pain. (Because the Biafran government is not recognized by any major country, Biafra is denied legal access on the international market to, among other things, morphine.) In terms of statistics, loss of life, displacement of persons, the war has already taken a greater toll than Vietnam; and yet people on the road inevitably return smiles, and life in this enormous ghetto under siege seems determined to proceed almost normally. As always in war, unless one happens to be at the front and be shot at, or caught in an air raid, there is nothing but symptoms—distortions of peace—to give one a sense of war and its losses. Premature or simply inaccurate Nigerian claims of areas captured have often sent observers to battle zones to find that they are not simply at the front —they *are* it; and four journalists have already been killed while reporting from the Nigerian side. But the strange image-consciousness of Biafrans makes them highly scrupulous about not sending reporters where Biafran soldiers have not arrived. Biafran information officials will try reporters with the strangest evasions, from subjects as knowable and precise as whether there is or is not a Biafran Telex (there is not), or whether there are in fact flights from Libreville, to subjects as hard to know in wartime as the exact population and casualty rate. But they are deeply concerned for the safety of foreigners. "Why do you choose to fly into this volcano?" an Ibo doctor, exhausted with work, asked a foreign visitor. "You have no right or obligation to die here." When the foreigner replied, "I think it is a shared right," the doctor said, "Thank you." There is everywhere this crazed, articulate, sometimes even irritable courtesy (Biafran speakers even tend to sound alike), in the face of an absolute desolation closing in.

Foreigners flying into Biafra now bring their own food and, if the pilot permits it, their own gasoline in jerry cans. What fuel there is in Biafra is made in little roadside refineries, which consist of a thatched hut over firewood and an arrangement of pipes and steel drums beside a brook, like a still. A loss of fuel can be as dire in Biafra now as the shortage of food, since the army must be mobile to reach any stress point on the completely encircling front. The symptoms of war are evident in everything from the sound of mortars miles from the front to the fact that all markets have moved under camouflage in the bush and that children at feeding centers can get only one meal a day (under trees, before dawn, for fear of the MIGs), and yet one subject Biafrans hardly ever talk about is the front, the actual progress of the war. Asked about this strange reticence, Biafrans will say the front is "irrelevant," or "We have no place to go. They take Owerri, we retake Umuahia. If we lose it all, we will fight without towns, from the bush." Another subject hardly mentioned in ordinary conversation, without laughter, is food, or even the starving of the children. If pressed, a Biafran will say he finds the subject "painful." Genocide, however, comes up again and again, and Biafrans will talk about a friend, a relative, a town, a personal flight from a mob before or in the war with a precise attention to dates and the most gruesome detail. Bombing raids on markets, churches, orphanages, and hospitals are recounted by families and in palm-wine bars with a kind of awe of their modern European quality, as though by dying on purely ethnic grounds Biafrans had established their place in modern history. One thing one hardly sees in Biafra is cemeteries. The dead are buried all over the third of the country that remains.

REPORT FROM THE FEDERAL SIDE [4]

On the federal side of the Nigerian struggle many people seem unaware that a war is going on. There are, of course, minor discomforts—the nightly blackout in Lagos; the unavailability of cars, Scotch whiskey and textiles; the increase in prices; and the soldiers, who demand bribes from civilians and push them around.

But in general, the discomforts of war are minor. Obese men in enormous robes can still be seen scattering chips across the roulette tables at the Federal Palace Hotel. Nigerian businessmen are getting rich, for the restriction of imports is bolstering local industry and oil production is near prewar level.

There are, of course, tensions and economic dislocations within Nigeria, but they are minor compared to conditions in Biafra, and Nigeria should be able to absorb them easily while still carrying on the war. Yet comparing conditions in the two regions may be pointless, for Nigerians may be unwilling to take as much as the Biafrans and may be more hurt by minor dislocations than Biafra is by major dislocations. Since assessing the will of the people and their capacity for discomfort is almost impossible, all one can say is that Nigeria *looks* very strong to a visitor.

The area of Nigeria seemingly least affected by the war is the old Northern Region. Yet changes have occurred there in the last few years that may affect the future stability of the country and be as vital to Nigeria in the long run as the course of the fighting in Biafra. Biafran Ibos were skeptical when in May 1967 Lieutenant Colonel Yakubu Gowon

[4] Article, "The Nigeria Which Is Not at War," by Stanley Meisler, correspondent for the Los Angeles *Times. Africa Report.* 15:16-17. Ja. '70. Reprinted by permission from Africa Report Magazine.

abolished the old federal system of four regions and divided the country into twelve states (six in the North). They were convinced that the split was merely formal and that in reality the old North remained united and powerful, ready to dominate Nigeria and slap down the Ibos again should they ever return.

Is There a New North?

But is there a new North? Has the monolithic, authoritarian structure of the old Northern Region cracked? Is separatism dead and Nigerian nationalism awake? Can the Ibos ever come back? Nigerian officials smugly reply yes to all these questions, but the answers are, in fact, elusive and contradictory. Northern officials insist that the division of the country is real and permanent, and certainly Kwara State, which is Yoruba-speaking, and Benue Plateau State, which is heavily Christian, are free from domination by the rest of the North, which is largely Hausa-speaking and dominated by Muslim Fulani emirs.

The other four states of the North also seem satisfied with the country's division. For years, the leaders of Kano, for example, felt shortchanged by the Sardauna of Sokoto in North-Western State. Now, with the division of the North, Kano has its own state and can pursue its own interests.

Yet it would be misleading to consider the division of the North permanent at this stage. Colonel Abba Kyari, military governor of North-Central State, has said that being divided into separate states would not prevent people from thinking alike. Certainly if the Muslim Hausas and their Fulani rulers ever felt threatened by an outside force, their four states could easily unite into a Muslim state almost as powerful and monolithic as the old Northern Region.

Still, there is talk of a new North, run by new men instead of by the emirs. And there is some evidence that the emirs' power is diminishing. The military governors of the six Northern states have appointed civilian commissioners to head the state ministries—several of them progressive, educated Northerners who have resisted the authority of the emirs in the past. In four of the states the institution of "chiefs in council" has been replaced by a governor-appointed local council, in which the emir, as chairman, has only one vote.

Another change that has come about in the North during the past few years is the influx of Yorubas, who have replaced the Ibos as Northern Nigeria's clerks, foremen, businessmen and teachers. The Northerners, who once regarded Ibos as foreign invaders, now see the Yorubas in the same light.

A year ago, rumors swept through Kano and Kaduna that the Hausas intended to slaughter the Yorubas just as the Ibos were slaughtered three years ago. Firm talk by the military governors and the emirs, however, calmed the Hausas, and the massacre never materialized. But tension still remains, and most state governments in the North prefer hiring white foreigners to Nigerian Yorubas. Despite this ethnic tension, Northern officials still speak of "one Nigeria," and there is no separatist talk. As long as the federal government poses no threat to the traditional North, the North will probably accept the present structure, for Gowon is a Northerner—although a Christian and a minority tribesman—and Northerners have no cause to chafe under his rule.

As for the future of the Ibos in the North, there is too little evidence to reach a conclusion. The state governments are collecting rents for Ibo property and promise to return both the property and the money to the Ibos when they come back. So far, a handful of Ibos have returned to claim their property and this small number has caused no problem. But a return of thousands might. The question of Ibos and Ibo property, like the question of Northern power and Northern separatism, can probably not be settled until after the war.

Disruptions in the West

Nigeria's most dramatic disruptions recently have occurred in the West. It has been estimated that more than two hundred people have been killed in clashes between agitators and the authorities since September 16 [1969], when farmers rushed the prison in Ibadan and released more than four hundred persons arrested for failure to pay taxes.

Biafrans were elated by the news of these clashes. At the time of their secession, the Ibos were counting on the Yorubas forming a separate state of their own. Chief Obafemi Awolowo's support of the federal government was regarded as treachery by shocked Biafrans. Now, some Biafrans have revived their old hopes: Biafran independence founded on the foundering of the West.

But the Biafran hope is overblown. Without doubt, the inconveniences of war have contributed to the West's troubles. Taxes and the cost of goods are higher. While cocoa commands higher prices in the world market, little of the profit goes to the Yoruba farmer, since the government keeps most of the extra revenue to pay for munitions. Traders must even bribe soldiers to get their trucks past roadblocks.

But in many ways the violence is tied less to disgruntlement with the war than to echoes of the past. The Yorubas are playing out the old Akintola-Awolowo rivalry again (Chief S. L. Akintola, the Western premier until his assassination in 1966, was opposed by Chief Obafemi Awolowo, president of the Action Group Party) and much of the rioting is aimed at discrediting Colonel Robert Adebayo and forcing the federal military government to split the Western State in two. The old rivalry is played out with more sophisticated weapons these days because the war has left so many modern guns around.

In a sense the West can afford the luxury of bitter political strife because it feels so aloof from the war. There is no compulsion to bury differences for the good of the war effort. But Nigeria's 150,000-man army (of which 12,000 troops are stationed in Ibadan) can handle the troubles in the West without slackening its latest offensive in Biafra, and the riots in the West are probably more indicative of Nigeria's instability after the war than of the course of the war itself.

One sign of Nigeria's inner strength is the story of oil production and the Biafran campaign against it. In April, oil production was going so well that Nigerian officials and foreign oil executives talked optimistically of reaching a production level of one million barrels a day by the end of the year. (Production had reached almost 600,000 barrels a day in April.) But then Biafra began attacking Nigerian oil installations, reducing oil production to 470,000 barrels a day by August. However, the Nigerians managed to get through the first year of the war with a much smaller oil production, and they can surely fight without strain on the revenue from 470,000 barrels a day—a royalty of perhaps $3.5 million a month.

The most depressing aspect of life in Nigeria is the atmosphere created by military rule. The soldiers are arrogant and bullying, for the army's enormous growth has come at the cost of discipline and training. Gone is the image of the honest soldier who seizes power to save the country from the corruption of politicians. The black Mercedes of the politicians have been replaced by the khaki Mercedes of the soldiers, and officers have made fortunes in bribery, looting and profiteering. Although the politicians continue to influence policy, they are despairing of ever returning to full power. Gowon has promised to return to the barracks once the war is over—but politicians are skeptical.

The tension in the North, the troubles in the West, the reduction in oil production, the malaise of military rule— all contribute to a certain weakening of spirit and morale in that part of Nigeria not directly involved in fighting the war. But Nigeria has held together fairly well during these many months of civil war, and these problems are not enough to enervate the war effort or split the country while the war is going on.

FOREIGN POWERS AND THE WAR [5]

Throughout the Nigerian war, both sides were convinced that foreign powers were the origin of their misfortunes—and it was characteristic that one of General [Yakubu] Gowon's first utterances after it was over should have been a warning against the return of "foreign meddlers." Colonel [Odumegwu] Ojukwu interpreted the war as a British neocolonialist venture, supported by the Russians because they needed a foothold in West Africa. The Nigerians did not see the origin of Biafra's secession as anywhere outside Biafra, but they were, and remain, convinced that outsiders—especially the French, the Portuguese, the South Africans and the Catholic Church—deliberately kept the war going for their own ends.

Far from instigating the war, outside powers were frequently baffled by it. Most British officials were taken by surprise by the January 1966 coup which started the train of events leading to war. When Biafra seceded, the Russians assumed it was Katanga all over again, with Anglo-Dutch oil interests taking the place of Union Minière and instigating the secession. When the French stepped in—strongly, as it turned out—with their belated support, they assumed Biafra would be able to hold out. The only serious argument that foreigners actually instigated the war was the Biafran view that without British encouragement the federals would have had neither the will nor the means to go to war. But in any event, it was federal determination to "keep Nigeria one" which proved the key factor: federal motivation was every bit as real as the Biafran.

If foreign powers cannot be said to have started the war, they did play a crucial role in its course and outcome. British arms were important, but Nigeria could probably have gotten them elsewhere; more significant was British political

[5] From "Foreign Powers and the Nigerian War: The Motives Behind British, French and Soviet Military Involvement—the Anticipated Versus the Actual Payoffs," by Walter Schwarz, African correspondent for *The Guardian* (London). *Africa Report*. 15:12-14. F. '70. Reprinted by permission from Africa Report Magazine.

and diplomatic support, which may well have been decisive in discouraging African and other nations from recognizing Biafra, in opposing the churches' nocturnal airlift, and in persuading the United States not to take an independent line. And without French arms and the food provided by the churches, Biafra could not have lasted as long as it did.

Britain's Policy

Britain's role has been a unique mixture of intrigue, bewilderment, disingenuousness and ruthlessness. The first significant involvement followed the second coup of July 1966, when the country was on the verge of breaking up. British High Commissioner Sir Francis Cumming-Bruce played an important role—along with the Lagos civil servants whose patriotism and self-interest made them the strongest force for unity—in persuading General Gowon not to carry through the original aim of the Northern coup leaders, which was secession of the North.

Britain's starting position, then, was a commitment to keep Nigeria from sliding apart by accident. When secession and war loomed, the line became more equivocal for a time. British journalists have tended to depict Whitehall as assuming that when war came there would be a "quick kill" for Lagos. But in retrospect this may have been a distortion, due specifically to the inane overoptimism and anti-Ibo (indeed anti-African) sentiments of a British information officer in Lagos who was later promoted to a higher information job in Whitehall. In fact, behind this facile facade, British officials had made a more realistic assessment of how long it might take Nigeria's tiny army, demoralized by two coups and deprived of its staff officers and technicians who were largely Ibo, to fight a modern war.

To oppose a threatened breakup of Nigeria in July 1966 was one thing; to side deliberately with Nigeria in its war and diplomatic effort against Biafra was another. It took some time for that policy to develop. As late as January 1968, Lord Shepherd, Minister of State at the Foreign Office, could tell the House of Lords: "We are neutral to both sides . . . we certainly are not helping one side or the other." Lord Shepherd was able then to justify the continued provision of arms to Lagos with the argument that this was a traditional supply, and that to halt it would have amounted to recognition and active help for Biafra. . . .

As federal victory proved elusive and the sufferings of the Biafrans increased, the government came under increasing pressure to justify its policy—and it was only then that the policy came to be formulated logically. The first argument was that Britain had no alternative: to stop arms to Lagos would not end the war but only antagonize Lagos. Allied to this was the feeling that Britain had created the federation as a showpiece of independence and had a residual responsibility to help preserve it. There was also the "liberal" view that Africa had to have some large and potentially powerful units if the continent were to make real progress. A more realistic argument was that Britain's formidable business interests in Nigeria would flourish only if the single large unit, with its uniquely large market, were preserved. Sudden withdrawal of support from Lagos might have meant confiscation, nationalization or other retribution. A fifth point was that since the Russians were already involved in aiding Lagos, British withdrawal would hand over Nigeria to them. But perhaps the most potent argument was that there was no workable alternative for Nigeria. "Biafra" was not Iboland alone, but it contained five million persons of other tribes who had shown few signs of wanting to be part of Biafra. After much Biafran territory had been recaptured by the federals, the limits of "Biafra" were so uncertain that allowing it to survive would have invited fresh wars, if not disintegration of the whole federation.

Mounting criticism in the press and Parliament challenged most, if not all, of these arguments. The "continuity" argument was challenged on the ground that in July 1966 the federation had in fact already broken apart, since the second coup had never been effective in the East. How could commercial interests flourish in a federation perennially disrupted by strife? As for the Russians, it was continuation of the war, not compromise with Biafra, that threatened to perpetuate both their presence and influence in Nigeria.

As the Biafran lobby and the hostile press stepped up their attacks, pressure on the prime minister became almost overwhelming. In the House of Commons, critical motions gained more than a hundred signatories in both parties—though party discipline ensured that less than that number actually voted against the government.

France's Role

The French seemed to come later onto the scene, but, in reality, when General de Gaulle announced in July 1968 that Biafra had a right to "self-determination," French policy was already well established. The sequence of events is still obscure; especially as to whether Ivory Coast President Félix Houphouët-Boigny persuaded de Gaulle (as French official sources claim) or whether it was the other way around. . . .

De Gaulle came into the open in July 1968. An announcement after a cabinet meeting said that "by the bloodshed and sufferings endured for over a year, the population of Biafra has demonstrated its will to assert itself as a people. . . . The French government considers that the conflict must be resolved on the basis of the right of peoples to self-determination and must include the setting in motion of appropriate international procedures." The last phrase was a clear hint that France at least contemplated following the Ivory Coast, Gabon, Tanzania and Zambia in recognizing Biafra. The debate on recognition was to continue even after de Gaulle's departure, but the step was never actually taken.

French motives were as complex and mixed, and in places as obscure, as the British. The only one which was officially admitted was humanitarian. This should not be dismissed entirely as camouflage, since French public opinion was aroused about Biafran sufferings long before the same thing

happened in Britain. A deeper motive was de Gaulle's phi-
losophy of nationalism and national self-assertion as exemplified in his resistance to American domination of Europe
and in his encouragement of separatist feeling in Quebec.
In colonial days France, like Britain, had large federations
in Africa. But it took the opposite course in decolonization,
and the federations of West Africa (Afrique Occidentale
Française) and Central Africa (Afrique Equatoriale Française) were broken up into their component parts before
independence. Britain's federal experiment in Nigeria was
watched with skepticism, then with jealousy when it seemed
to be succeeding, and finally with *schadenfreude* when it
broke apart. At the purely political level, de Gaulle must
have felt that the British were making a fatal mistake in
supporting Lagos with arms in what looked like a war which
could not be won, and seen in this an opportunity for France
to embarrass Britain and at the same time gain political
and economic advantages. Nigeria's inordinate size and potential wealth, especially after the discovery of oil, also
posed a geopolitical threat to the tiny countries in the
French orbit.

Economic motives are necessarily more obscure. On balance, the preponderance of French commercial interests was
on the federal side. Even the oil deposits of the former
Eastern Region were mostly out of Biafran control by the
time French support became crucial. However, since France
is short of oil it is scarcely conceivable that oil played no
part in French motivation. The calculation might well have
been that if Biafra survived it would eventually regain its
former boundaries, which included rich reserves. No detailed
evidence of any Franco-Biafran oil deal has come to light,
and thus this must remain a matter of speculation.

In the later stages of the war, President Pompidou did
not change the official line—and even after the fall of Biafra
the French government stated (perhaps not very helpfully,
in view of the Ibos' current plight) that Biafra would once
again press its right of self-determination. However, there

was evidence that aid to Biafra was limited and that there was no open-ended commitment. A profederal commercial lobby had made itself felt in Paris, and Biafra was never given an equivalent of the long-range Soviet artillery, jet planes, or British armored vehicles which were decisive in the federal military advantage. Having sustained a cause which they finally allowed to perish at terrible human cost, the fall of Biafra left the French in as indefensible a moral position as the British.

Russian Motives

Soviet involvement began from what looked like an honest mistake. Since it was the oil-rich East which seceded, Soviet analysts followed the Katanga parallel and assumed that oil interests were secretly intriguing to detach the oil from a Nigeria that might prove too demanding. This theory seemed all the more plausible when Shell-BP [Shell-British Petroleum] and other oil companies provisionally decided to pay Ojukwu $20 million in royalties. But the Russians were totally wrong. The oil companies were alarmed and apprehensive about secession from the state, and the decision to pay the royalties arose from the *force majeure* situation. There was no parallel with Katanga except insofar as French support for both secessions may have had similar motives. The oil companies, in fact, became active supporters of the federal cause—especially when new discoveries changed the emphasis from the East to the Mid-West and off-shore sources.

The Soviet opportunity came when Britain proved hesitant in providing arms of the type and on the scale demanded. Soviet MIGs played a larger part in the deliberate bombing of Biafran civilians—thereby harming federal Nigeria's image and attracting sympathy for Biafra—than in the fighting itself. But the heavy artillery with a range of thirteen miles which was supplied in the final stage of the war may well have been decisive.

Soviet motives were transparent enough. Russia has long needed a new presence in West Africa after its disappointments in Guinea and Ghana. . . . Nigeria had been the biggest prize all along, yet it was the most difficult of access for the Russians. Its first civilian regime was controlled by Northern politicians who could not have been more conservative and more suspicious of the Russians, and the Russian diplomatic and economic presence was deliberately kept to a minimum. After the 1966 coups, the situation hardly improved, since the Sandhurst-trained officers were even further to the right. Overnight, the war changed the situation. In the need to please the Russians in exchange for arms, the federal government eased restrictions in all spheres. For the first time Soviet cars were assembled in Nigeria and an import license system was inaugurated to ensure that they made their impact on the market. The iron and steel project, the biggest single venture on Nigerian drawing boards, was entrusted to the Russians. But most vital from the Soviet point of view, the arms and other projects opened the way to a massive influx of advisers and technicians. Nigerian-Soviet friendship societies flourished, and politicians and trade-union leaders long friendly to the Russians were deliberately given their head, and Nigerian students left in large numbers for Moscow.

Had the war dragged on through 1970 and beyond, the Russian presence in Nigeria might have become permanent. But with the end of the war, the federal government is likely to view it, and all new overtures, with caution. Now that it has won the war, Nigeria is likely to keep all foreigners at arm's length for quite some time.

THE END OF BIAFRA [6]

All along, it had been more of an atrocity than a war. For every soldier slain in a jungle skirmish, scores of men, women and children had slowly starved in the shrinking

[6] From "Biafra: End of a Lost Cause." *Newsweek*. 75:48-50+. Ja. 26, '70. Copyright Newsweek, Inc., January 26, 1970. Reprinted by permission.

confines of their wasted tribal homeland. And as the outside world watched in helpless horror, a proud nation sacrificed perhaps two million of its people in a hopeless cause. Yet when the Nigerian civil war came to an abrupt conclusion last week, it did so in a courtly tableau reminiscent of Appomattox. In a magnanimous gesture, federal Nigeria's victorious leader, Major General Yakubu Gowon, extended a soldierly welcome to Biafra's Chief of Staff, Major General Philip Effiong, at Dodan Barracks in Lagos. "We are loyal Nigerian citizens," Effiong promised in return. "The Republic of Biafra hereby ceases to exist." Then, amid a round of champagne and self-conscious bear hugs, Gowon jubilantly exclaimed: "We have been reunited with our brothers."

For Gowon, the moment was one to be savored. His chief antagonist, Biafra's General Odumegwu Ojukwu, had flown off to ignominious exile somewhere in Europe. And with that, the war that many people had thought unwinnable ended in a resounding triumph for Yakubu Gowon. But throughout the rest of the world, the end of the civil war brought no sense of relief. For out in the trackless bush were hundreds of thousands of frightened Biafran refugees and, despite some evidence to the contrary, many observers believed that these hapless victims of the war were on the brink of starvation. It was upon the refugees' plight that most of the world's attention focused. Pope Paul VI lamented: "One fear torments public opinion—the fear that the victory of arms may carry with it the killing of numberless people. There are those who actually fear a kind of genocide."

Understandable as it was, this wave of international concern struck many Nigerians as presumptuous meddling. For the moment, at least, Nigeria had emerged from the crucible of civil war with a new sense of pride, power and nationhood. And in his hour of victory, Gowon was not about to be pushed around. Even as cargo planes stuffed with food and medicines waited on tarmacs around the world, the Nigerian leader bluntly announced that when he wanted help he would ask for it. Insisting that Nigeria would set its own house in order, Gowon rejected most early offers of assistance, thus raising the grim possibility that more thousands of Biafrans might die before help reached them. More than anything else, this attitude served notice on the great powers that black Africa's most populous nation no longer considered itself anyone's client state.

Ban on Aid

No sooner had the war ended than Gowon's military regime announced that it would accept no aid from France, Portugal, South Africa or Rhodesia—nations that, in one way or another, had supported the Ibo tribesmen who ruled Biafra. Also blacklisted were the international relief agencies that had flown supplies into Biafra from the Portuguese island of São Tomé during the wartime blockade; these groups included Joint Church Aid, an interdenominational agency, and Caritas, the Roman Catholic relief organization. "Let them keep their blood money," Gowon said in an interview on the Nigerian radio. "We don't want it. We will do it ourselves, and I want to assure you of this: we *will* do it."

This stubborn self-reliance reflected Nigeria's deep resentment over the aid and sympathy that Biafra had received from some governments and from many private individuals even in nations that officially supported Nigeria. To many on the federal side, the ranking *bête noire* was the Catholic Church. In a statement issued shortly after the shooting stopped, the Lagos government charged the Vatican with "sustaining the rebels with money and vital supplies and transportation links with the outside world." The role of the Vatican, the statement continued, "has had the tragic consequence of prolonging rebel resistance, leading to the deaths of many innocent people." And in the exuberant demonstrations set off by word of Biafra's surrender, one Lagos marcher put the case more succinctly with a placard that proclaimed: "Hottest part of hell for the Pope!"

Nigeria was even suspicious of its loyal friends. "We in Nigeria, more than anyone else in the world, have been compelled to grasp the meaning and repulsive nature of Western humanitarianism in all its guises," a government-owned newspaper, *The New Nigerian,* declared in an editorial. "We now know that Western humanitarianism is no more than an instrument for subverting the self-respect of its object." Thus, the British, Nigeria's senior patrons, were coolly told that a Royal Air Force transport plane that had been standing by outside London with a cargo of relief supplies might just as well be unloaded. And the United States, whose diplomats had staunchly—if quietly—supported Nigerian unity, was rebuffed when it offered to send planes and helicopters from Pope Air Force Base in North Carolina. In no uncertain terms, Gowon let it be known that he had no intention of allowing Nigeria to be overrun by military planes, pilots and crews from Western countries. "By keeping the relief efforts securely in Nigerian hands," said a U.S. official, "Gowon is playing to his country's xenophobia. A lot of white faces running about the countryside could be his political undoing."

Gowon's difficulties were compounded by the fact that no one knew for sure just how many people remained in the former Biafran heartland—or just how badly off they were. Most official estimates placed the total number of refugees at around 3.5 million, of whom between 1 million and 2 million people were thought to be in dire need of food. Relief workers who flew out of Biafra just before the collapse told a story of chaos and imminent famine. By the tens of thousands, fleeing civilians clogged the roads in all directions, and according to some reports, ravenous Biafran soldiers were using their weapons to obtain food. The last relief planes to take off from beleaguered Uli airstrip, Biafra's main link with the outside world during the last year of the thirty-month war, were engulfed by desperate refugees, and one of the craft was riddled with machine-gun fire when it left.

Against this Goyaesque background officials of the relief agencies warned that, without further mercy flights from São Tomé, mass starvation was imminent. "Hundreds of thousands could die in a few days," said the Reverend Nicholas Frank, the deputy director of Caritas. "The physical resistance of the people is zero. Anyone who does not eat for one or two days is finished." No one doubted the gigantic proportions of the crisis. Like many observers, however, the relief workers saw the situation from their own passionately committed point of view. And it was worth bearing in mind that, for the most part, they had served in those Biafran areas hit hardest by famine.

The Nigerians, for their part, insisted that they had the situation well in hand. They calculated that some 13,000 tons of emergency food supplies were stockpiled in Nigeria itself, with another 7,000 tons on the way. This, they said, would amply meet the demand—9,000 tons a month to feed the 2 million people—without using foods stored on São Tomé and elsewhere. Moreover, Gowon had not shut the door to all foreign aid. The United States and Britain were contributing about $12 million each in fresh financial assistance, both directly and through the United Nations, and other Western countries were also chipping in. And in order to prevent panic among the Biafrans—many of whom still expected to be slaughtered—federal troops halted their advance into rebel territory. By . . . [January 17, 1970], Chief Anthony Enahoro, the Lagos government's spokesman, reported Nigerian relief teams were already feeding 700,000 people, and supplementing the diets of 1 million more. By his account, the emergency would be over in a month.

Partial support for that view came from an observer team composed of military officers from Canada, Poland, Sweden and Britain. The observers punctured one balloon by reporting that they "neither saw nor heard of any evidence of genocide" in the newly conquered areas. And they said that the refugees flowing out of the battle zones for the most part "appeared to be in good physical shape." "There were some children who seemed to have malnutrition, with their big bellies," said Major General Yngve Berglund of Sweden. "But they were walking, so they could not have been so badly off."

The observers' report, however, was less than conclusive. For the parts of Biafra visited by the officers contained less than 150,000 refugees and, with only one exception, had long been in federal hands. Disturbingly, the observers were unable to visit the areas hardest hit by famine. And until the beginning of this week, none of the 250 foreign newsmen who had flocked to Nigeria were permitted to visit the battle zone, with the result that as yet there was no independent confirmation of the observers' findings.

Sudden Debacle

One element that further complicated the relief effort was the fact that the war had ended with such unexpected suddenness, catching even the Nigerians unprepared for peace. When Biafra seceded in May 1967, the rebels faced an inept federal army of only 12,000 men, and for much of the following two and a half years both sides settled down to a torpid equatorial *sitzkrieg*. The Nigerian ranks rapidly expanded to some 120,000 men (as against roughly 40,000 on the Biafran side), and as the war dragged on, they were supplied with an increasingly potent arsenal of British and Soviet weapons, including armored cars, sophisticated artillery and MIG and Ilyushin warplanes manned by Egyptian pilots. But although the Biafrans were badly outnumbered and outgunned, they received just enough help from France and other foreign sources to hang on. The rebels gave ground grudgingly, and one "final offensive" after another by the clumsy federal forces fizzled in humiliating fashion.

Then, at Christmas, the Nigerian army surprised even its most optimistic well-wishers. With the Biafrans forced back into a kidney-shaped enclave barely a tenth of their nation's original size, the Nigerian Third Marine Commando Division, led by Lieutenant Colonel Olu Obasanjo, began a drive from the south and finally linked up with the First Division near Umuahia. This cut off a five-hundred-square-mile bulge from the rest of Biafra. Then the First Division proceeded to link up with the Second Division near Onitsha, and the rebel enclave was cut in three. More important, for the first time in the war, the federal forces controlled a network of roads that gave them complete freedom to maneuver around the Biafran defenses. And they had a powerful new weapon: a 122 mm. Russian field gun with a thirteen-mile range. Taking full advantage of all these assets, Obasanjo rolled up the Biafrans' southern front and sent Ojukwu fleeing for his life.

To the rebels, the sudden debacle was almost uncanny. Some Biafrans blamed their defeat on the activities of witch doctors in the Twelfth Biafran Division, which abruptly collapsed at a crucial moment. But the real explanation was much more mundane. "The Biafran resistance just sort of disintegrated," said a Catholic priest. "They seemed to run out of everything at the same time." On São Tomé, one fugitive from the Twelfth Division explained to *Newsweek*'s Marvin Kupfer that he had fled because "I was afraid and hungry. Some days we had only water. Sometimes, we had food only once in three days. How can you fight when you have no food?" In Libreville, the capital of neighboring Gabon, an Irish priest told *Newsweek*'s John Barnes that many soldiers had come begging at his clinic. "It used to break my heart to see the young kids," he said. "Some of them only seventeen, some of them my own former pupils, their ribs sticking out of their bodies—and we had to turn them away." By this point, morale was so low that the Biafran army had almost ceased to exist as a fighting force.

The same despair infected the civilian population. Recent arrivals on São Tomé . . . told Kupfer of desperate refugees pleading for food. "Help us, woman-fathers," they cried to nuns who passed them on the road. "But how could we help them?" said a sixty-one-year-old sister from America.

"They wouldn't listen to us. They wanted to run. They were afraid and we couldn't blame them. They just kept coming from everywhere." One of the last white women to leave Biafra was Davida Taylor, thirty-one, an American doctor who had returned to her clinic from abroad only weeks before:

> The biggest change I found was that people could no longer take the war [she said]. They talked of peace at any cost and any risk. I continually heard things like, "Nothing can be worse than this," or, "If Ojukwu is really a great man, he will surrender." People would exchange stories about Nigerian troops capturing an area and treating everyone kindly. The big Christmas offensive, when it came, was just the final straw.

For many Biafrans, the end was signaled when Obasanjo's men captured the mobile transmitters of Radio Biafra, which for thirty months had rallied the people of the secessionist state. Seizing a microphone, Obasanjo announced that his forces were "garrisoned throughout the Eastern State," and he instructed Biafran troops to hand in their weapons to the nearest federal unit. After the announcement, the station, which had identified itself as Radio Biafra just before Obasanjo went on the air, hurriedly renamed itself "Radio Nigeria," and in place of the slow threnody of classical music that had been its main output since Ojukwu took to his heels, the station broke out with a lighthearted selection of popular tunes. . . .

To many people abroad, Biafra's final collapse came not only as a surprise but as a tragedy. Throughout its thirty-one months of precarious existence, the secessionist state was the focus of intense emotions. It attracted a huge and diverse international following, partly because it embodied so many causes. To some people, the issue seemed primarily religious, for while many Ibos are devout Catholics, the rest of Nigeria is dominated by Muslim tribes from the North. Other outsiders took Biafra's part out of sheer pity, while still others viewed the secessionists as brave underdogs or gallant fighters for self-determination.

AFTERMATH OF WAR: AN IBO'S VIEW [7]

Shortly after Nigeria's bloody civil war came to a sudden end six months ago, foreign journalists were taken on a supervised tour of the defeated Eastern Region, where rebellious Ibo tribesmen had lost out in their thirty-month struggle for an independent Biafra. The journalists found widespread evidence of famine, but few signs of the vengeful bloodbath that Ibo leaders had feared. Since then, few Westerners have gained access to the war-ravaged area, and the outside world has heard little of how Ibos are faring. To gauge the current situation, *Newsweek* asked a former rebel, now working in Enugu, capital of the Eastern Region, for his impressions of life today. Here is his report, which for his own protection is unsigned:

The war has left its scars, but Enugu is still a city with lovely vistas, and life here as elsewhere in the Eastern Region is slowly returning to normal. Heaps of refuse that had been piling up over the last three years are finally being cleared away. Shops are putting their old signboards back up and dabbing a little paint here and there whenever the owners can afford it. In the morning you see crowds of people going to work, to the market, to business. The streets are no less thronged in the evening, as people visit friends and relatives or stop for a pleasant hour at one of the many drinking centers. Men cluster around the little open-air snack shops, with their bottles of palm wine standing on rickety tables. The talk is mostly casual—about women and their micro-mini frocks which our parents feel are outraging our native culture; about when the railway will restore service; about whether the national bank will ever exchange our Biafran currency; about the new taxes. Occasionally the conversation will turn to Gowon [Major General Yakubu Gowon, the Nigerian chief of state], but nobody seems very interested in politics these days.

[7] Article, "Life in What Was 'Biafra': An Ibo's View." *Newsweek.* 76:37. Jl. 20, '70. Copyright Newsweek, Inc., July 20, 1970. Reprinted by permission.

Hungry

What concerns the average Ibo is how to stay alive and make ends meet. There is no denying that a lot of people are still hungry. Many workers are waiting for reinstatement to their old jobs, and others are hoping for new ones. Some eat once, others twice a day. Last week a policeman from my block, who had visited police headquarters every day asking for a job, collapsed and died of hunger in his home. In some rural areas I have visited, the situation is even worse. People are dying daily from hunger, and many cases of kwashiorkor [a disease stemming from protein deficiency] are again being treated in hospitals. There are no more breadlines because the Red Cross recently closed down its relief center here, but schoolchildren still queue up once or twice a week for a free glass of milk.

We know some more of us will die, but we are tired of hearing about it. The attitude of most Ibos seems to be that nothing worse can happen than has already happened, so we must take life as it comes. There are certainly no plans —at least on the part of anyone I know—for organizing any kind of resistance. Today, Ibos are not thinking of making trouble. A lot of planting has been done since the big rains began in April, and we all hope for a bumper harvest next fall. As one farmer told me: "Thank God there are no soldiers and hungry thieves to ravage my farm any more."

There are many fellow Nigerians who are welcoming us back like brothers. But there are also many who are not happy about the return of the Ibos to the Nigerian fold. Oddly enough, it is in the Northern and Western Regions, where Ibos had so much trouble before the war, that we are being accepted again rather warmly. It appears that a reconciliation between the Ibos and Northern tribes like the Hausas, which we once thought impossible, may yet come about. But it may take decades for the wounds to heal in the war zone itself. It is no secret that our relations with other tribes in the Eastern Region are very poor. Ibos cannot travel to places like Port Harcourt in the Rivers State or to Calabar, Uyo and Ikot Ekpene in the South-Eastern State without fear of being attacked, and local authorities in those areas have barred many Ibos from returning to their jobs.

Personally, it took me about a month to accept the fact that the war had been lost. Since that time I have been steadily trying to reconvince myself that I am a Nigerian. In my student days, I used to write articles favoring Nigerian unity. Now, sometimes I reflect on what I used to preach—but sometimes I still feel I am a "Biafran" living in Nigeria. It is true that we have been on the losing side, but frankly I don't feel humiliated. I feel instead that it was a great feat for the rebel forces to have held out the way they did. Few outsiders, moreover, seem to understand our feelings about Odumegwu Ojukwu [the former Biafran rebel leader now living in exile in the Ivory Coast]. If Ojukwu had been caught by the federal army and tortured to death, this would have greatly aggravated the bitterness of many Ibos, who would have felt equally humiliated. Because he managed to escape, it is easier for us to settle down now as Nigerians.

And I still feel that, despite the war, my people will recover and Nigeria—with our help—will become a great nation in Africa. Some Nigerians say that the war should have taught us Ibos a lesson. But I rather think all Nigerians should now learn a lesson. African tribes should be able to merge into larger units—into nations—despite cultural and religious differences. I do not consider it in keeping with modern political thought for each tribe to form its own city-state. On the other hand, it remains to be seen whether this thing called "Nigeria" can stay together. I think the Ibos are ready to give it a chance. As our regional administrator and temporary spokesman, Ukpabi Asika, said recently: "It may be and is true that our people are bitter, angry and resentful. It is nonetheless our obligation to lead them away from anger, resentment and bitterness to accommodation, good neighborliness and amity." As long as we are treated as second-raters and are held down, we will dream of independence. But right now we are only thinking of how to stay alive.

PROBLEMS OF RECONSTRUCTION [8]

The process of reconciliation between Biafran and federal supporters had a good send-off with General Yakubu Gowon publicly and warmly embracing General Philip Effiong, commander of the defeated forces. It was a moving occasion, but the testing time for Nigeria's unity is still to come. The country is headed into a period of turbulent, perhaps even violent, politics, which could last for as long as the civil war and possibly even longer.

The war itself solved none of the problems on which the old Nigeria finally broke up. It proved only the tenacity of purpose of diverse peoples to stay together for their mutual advantage, and the tenacity of the Ibos in their desire not to be dominated or threatened by others.

We are unlikely ever to know exactly how many Ibos and other Nigerians died in the struggle. Some put the figure at over two million. My own guess is that this will turn out to be a fictional figure designed for propaganda purposes. It may be a million. But what a price to pay for a cause that was doomed almost from the start, an unnecessary war over a problem that was always politically negotiable.

Nevertheless, the fears that led the Ibos into an act of almost national suicide are shared in varying degrees by the two other major national groups, the Yorubas and the Hausas, as well as by scores of minority tribes who comprise a substantial part of Nigeria's ... [population].

As in all countries with diverse ethnic and cultural groups, the root of the problem has all along been the difficulty of achieving a political system capable of satisfying two often contradictory needs. Somehow, a high degree of

[8] Article by Colin Legum, Commonwealth correspondent of *The Observer* (London). *Current.* 116:47-51. Mr. '70. Taken from his article "After the Tragedy" which appeared in the January 18, 1970, issue of *The Observer.* Copyright, *The Observer.* Reprinted with permission of the Los Angeles Times/Washington Post News Service.

local autonomy must be combined with a central authority strong enough to promote national interests. It is a problem that plagues countries as diverse as India, Pakistan, South Africa, Canada and Belgium—and even the United Kingdom.

In Nigeria the problem is rawer and more complex than in most countries (though it is not as severe as in South Africa). Here one is up against the difficulty of striking a balance among three strong national groups, none of which wants to be dominated by the other two, while the minorities want to be safeguarded against unfair domination by all three.

A Nation of States?

What makes the problem even more difficult is that none of the national groups is truly homogeneous. Thus the powerful Hausas in the North hanker after their own separate states. The Yorubas are divided between those living in the Western State, and even these are internally divided. Even the Ibos are no longer certain whether they wish to remain together in a single state.

No wonder that many argue in favor of simply allowing everybody to go their own way. What does it matter, it is asked, if countries like Nigeria or India split apart, so long as this makes everybody happier? This is precisely the difficulty: not everybody would be happier. Economically, most would suffer. Security would be at a premium. A fragmented Africa or Asia would not only perpetuate poverty and backwardness; it would make for a maximum of insecurity and conflicts between small, poor warring nations. Nigeria's problem is the problem of the modern world: its solution doesn't lie in eighteenth century ideas. There can be no going back. But can one be confident that it's possible to go forward? And where, in Nigeria's case, does going forward lie?

Those now in power in the federation are agreed on only one single objective: that Nigeria's future is to be found in creating a collection of states somehow linked together in a central government. Beyond this there is no consensus of opinion.

With the formal establishment of the new Central-Eastern State of Iboland there will be twelve such states: six in the old Hausa-dominated North; three in the old Yoruba-dominated West, and three in the old Ibo-dominated East. Nobody is wedded to a final figure of twelve states. There might well be fifteen or even eighteen. But to get agreement about which of the present dozen should be further split up is bound to lead to bitter controversy, possibly even violent conflict.

A Loose Federation?

Chief [Obafemi] Awolowo, the veteran Yoruba leader, is adamant that his people should not be further divided. But only the exigencies of war have so far thinly disguised the struggle already going on among the Yoruba, the outcome of which is hard to foretell. On the other hand, the leaders of the minorities are already banded together to prevent the reemergence of a political system which—as happened in the past—would allow the stronger groups to dominate the weaker.

This conflict over the future shape of the states is by no means the only difficulty, possibly not even the most critical. A deeper conflict will be faced over the federal pattern into which the new states should be drawn. Here the line-up is between those who favor a strongly centralized federation (India is being cited as a possible model), and those who want a looser federation or even possibly a confederation of autonomous states. Even while the war was going on the politicians were quietly lining up their supporters and planning their strategy for when the political struggle over constitution-making would resume. That time has now come.

It should be clear that Nigeria is not going to slip easily from war into peace. Tranquillity is still a long way off. The outstanding asset in the troubles that lie ahead is the quiet, modest and widely respected figure of General Yakubu Gowon, a humane soldier so far almost entirely untouched by any desire for personal power or by any wish to perpetuate military rule for a day longer than it takes the politicians to reach agreement among themselves.

Gowon is a man of the North, which is under Islamic influence and dominated by the Hausas, but he is neither a Muslim nor a member of the Hausa people. He comes from a first-generation Christian family of the quite small Angwa tribe.

The Role of Minorities

After the two military coups in 1966, and the subsequent withdrawal of the Ibos to their own region, the comparatively few junior officers from the minority tribes unexpectedly found that they were in a position to play a key role in the army, which was then in control of the whole country.

In the midst of these upheavals, Gowon arrived home, daisy fresh from a training course, a gay, rather shy young bachelor (he married only recently), with a barely detectable stammer, a keen sportsman, an enthusiastic scouter and an efficient soldier. Literally overnight, at the age of thirty-two, he was selected by his fellow officers as the supreme military commander and head of a military regime struggling to hold together the crumbling and most populous state in the African continent.

What Future Army?

The army remains a worry. Inflated to 150,000 men not counting Biafrans, it is a Frankenstein's monster with a vested interest of its own. It is composed very largely of young unemployed school-leavers from the towns and underemployed peasants. The country simply can't afford to keep so many men under arms nor does its security require this. But neither can its security stand the consequences of simply sending these men, who have been schooled in violence, back into unemployment.

There are other seriously worrying problems as well. Nigeria's leaders, military and political, are fed up to their back teeth with the international involvements brought on by the war. They are sick of being lectured by friends and enemies, of having their intentions questioned at every point, of being accused that their standards of behavior may not live up to what the international community may demand.

Who, for God's sake, they ask, is the West, with its recent history of behavior to lecture them? They point with considerable justification to the fact that Nigeria is the first country in the world ever to have allowed foreign observers to hold a watching brief over how her soldiers behave. How would the Americans have reacted to a similar request in Vietnam, or the Russians in Czechoslovakia?

The Nigerians have responded to countless proposals to allow relief to flow into Biafra, even when it was clear that this aid was helping to sustain the morale of the Ibos. Not only did they agree to abide by the Geneva conventions of the Red Cross, Nigeria is the only country which has ever agreed to go beyond what those protocols require of a country at war.

Nigerians have seen the international relief organizations —largely the Christian churches—defy their authority and sustain Biafra's cause not only by providing relief but by supporting directly and indirectly the powerful anti-Nigerian lobbies which almost succeeded in swinging the Western countries against their cause.

Gowon is an honorable man, and as with most honorable men extremely touchy where his honor is concerned. Deeply influenced by Christian values, he has taken very badly the weight of criticism heaped on his regime by Christian leaders and organizations, and especially by the Roman Catholics.

The last straw was when the Pope in his latest appeal sought to reinject the long-exploded propaganda myth about genocide in his pontifical plea for tolerance. Who, the Nigerians ask, writes the Pope's messages to Lagos? They read like the utterances of the Biafran lobby, which has many far-right politicians and neocolonialists among its most convinced supporters. All this growing irritation has at last exploded into exasperated anger.

What Russian Influence?

Russian influence is not yet a major factor in Nigerian thinking about their future international relations, but it has grown a lot, especially and predictably among the young Northern radicals, who are emerging as a powerful new force from the decaying system of Muslim emirates. American influence, strong before the collapse of the old republic, is now almost at zero, the result of her ambiguous policies and her almost exclusive concern with relief to the neglect of Nigeria's national objectives. The French are despised by the federals because of their support for the Biafrans, and by the Ibos because of their failure to make good their promises.

Of all the Western countries only Britain has so far successfully survived the reassessment of international policy that has been going on throughout the war. But even the British have not come through unscathed. Their careful attempts to limit their supply of arms, which led the Nigerians to turn to the Russians in the first place, and their steady pressures on Nigerian leaders to make concessions, have produced a noticeable sense of irritation with Nanny England.

It is easy to understand the desire of the Nigerians, now that the war is over, to be left to themselves to put their own house in order. But in the coming struggle it's more than likely that the contesting groups will seek, when it suits their purposes, to enlist the support of powerful outside friends.

One is left with a last crucial question. Is it going to be possible for the Ibos to rejoin the Nigerian fold in the confident knowledge that they will not be made to pay for all that has happened in the past?

What Place for the Ibos?

The protagonists of Biafra's cause have argued all along that the Ibos could never again become part of a united Nigeria. They have been proved miserably wrong and misguided on a number of other contentions: that the Ibos could not be defeated militarily; that world opinion would never allow this to happen; that the Ibos would all die in the last ditch rather than submit; that even if the fighting front collapsed there would be years of guerrilla activity; that a federal victory would be followed by genocide.

Will they also be proved wrong about the future place of the Ibos in the new Nigeria? My view is that they will, that the Ibos will rejoin the Nigerian family, not without difficulty but without persecution, that eventually they will take their place in the new political struggle, finding their own allies in arguing for a looser rather than a strait-jacket federal system.

The old suspicions about their ambition and avarice and cleverness will persist, but these suspicions exist also about others. It was the Ibo instructors who rallied the Biafran army with the cry of "Kill the Hausas" when they must have known that the bulk of the federal forces were non-Hausa. The Yorubas, too, are being watched warily. Many of the minority tribes are suspicious of all three majority groups, and the majority groups feel they are being imposed upon by the minorities, who have a position of temporary dominance within the present military set-up.

These suspicions and fears are all part and parcel of what constitutes Nigeria's problems. The Ibos are only one aspect of the whole problem. To focus too exclusively on this talented, hapless people is to ignore the wider realities of Nigeria's complex society.

NIGERIA: THE SECOND DECADE [9]

The celebrations were scheduled to last a full week, and to ensure that a good time would be had by all, the Nigerian government decreed that workers be advanced a month's salary. Lagos, the capital, was decked out in flags and multicolored bunting, its streets swept clean, its buildings freshly painted and its hordes of beggars hustled out of sight. For

[9] From article in *Newsweek*. 76:44+. O. 5, '70. Copyright Newsweek, Inc., October 5, 1970. Reprinted by permission.

the comfort of visiting dignitaries, a Greek luxury liner had been brought in to serve as a floating hotel and a fleet of new Mercedeses had been assembled to haul the VIPs around in style. All these elaborate preparations may have seemed a trifle excessive to outsiders. But to Nigerians celebrating the tenth anniversary of their nation's independence this week, no amount of hoopla could do justice to one central fact: after a decade of turmoil and political dissension capped by a bloody civil war, Africa's most populous and potentially richest nation still hung together.

That was more than many experts had thought possible when, on October 1, 1960, Britain granted independence to its largest colony in Africa. Even the Nigerians themselves chose to celebrate that occasion with a notable measure of restraint. Aware of their country's vast tribal, linguistic and religious diversity, they sensed that the real tests of nationhood still lay ahead. And as things turned out, Nigeria's first decade of independence resulted in more murder and mayhem, more political assassinations and civil strife, than has befallen any other African country with the possible exception of the Congo. No one kept an accurate body count, but the two-and-a-half-year civil war waged by Ibo tribesmen on behalf of an independent Biafra is estimated to have cost at least 3 million lives—with more dying of starvation than of battle wounds.

Yet in the grim crucible of the Biafran conflict, Nigeria appears to have forged its first full measure of national consciousness and its first genuinely national political leaders, as well. "To make Nigeria one is a task that must be done" —such was the somewhat lumbering slogan of Major General Yakubu Gowon, the personable, thirty-five-year-old head of state who led Nigeria's federal forces to victory in the civil war . . . [in] January [1970]. Since then, Gowon has made the "three Rs" of relief, reconstruction and reconciliation his number one priority, and even skeptics agree that the return of the defeated Ibos to the national fold has gone forward with amazing smoothness. In the North, where opposition to

Biafran independence was strongest, Ibos have been trickling back apprehensively to regain some of their lost properties, and most have been pleasantly surprised by the welcome accorded them. In Enugu, the capital of the East-Central State and a onetime stronghold of Ibo resistance, former Biafrans and Nigerian soldiers jokingly call each other "vandals" (the Biafran term for federal troops) and "rebels"—and, despite predictions to the contrary, soldier-civilian relations seem good.

Meanwhile, Nigeria itself is moving to resume a more influential role in African affairs. General Gowon recently returned from a visit to four African states, including Egypt, and last month diplomatic relations with Tanzania, Zambia, Gabon and the Ivory Coast, each of which had recognized Biafra during the course of the civil war, were restored. There is no doubt that Soviet influence in Lagos has been growing (the Russians were prime suppliers to federal forces during the war), but the climate for private foreign investment remains good. And thanks in part to a strong capitalist streak in the Nigerian character, Gowon's flirtation with Moscow has in no way slowed the inflow of American and British aid. By skillful management, Gowon's advisers kept the country financially afloat throughout the war years, and with revenues from oil production spurting ahead (an estimated $280 million this year versus $78 million last year), foreign confidence in the economy is rapidly returning.

With peace restored and the economy moving back into gear, there is speculation that General Gowon will cap the independence-day celebrations this week by announcing a timetable for a return to democratic civilian rule within two or three years. [The target date is 1976.] But it is a measure of Gowon's personal prestige—and of the troubles that still plague his country—that few Nigerians seem overjoyed at that prospect. The nation remains fractionalized, with little in common between the Islamic, desert culture of the North and the animist and Christian traditions of the tropical

South. As a Northerner who is also a Christian, Gowon might seem a logical choice for the role of conciliator. But even he has been criticized by Northerners for showing more concern for the vanquished than the victors in the recent war.

Despite its economic potential, moreover, Nigeria is a desperately poor country, and there is no question but that the Ibos, once the most prosperous and still the most industrious of its peoples, are now among the worst off. Hunger and malnutrition are still rampant in the East-Central State, and in recent weeks disturbing reports have filtered out of the area indicating that food donated to orphanages by the Red Cross and medicines donated by UNICEF have been turning up on the black market. Jobs are now almost impossible to find in the East, and some former rebels have dug up their guns and begun terrorizing fellow Ibos just to stay alive. In fact, armed robbery has become a national phenomenon; recently the government decreed that such crimes be punished by public execution, and already one such spectacle has been held on the race course in Lagos.

Thus the puzzle of how to construct a viable, self-governing democracy out of Nigeria's . . . varied peoples remains to be solved. "Putting all considerations to the test —political, economic, as well as social," Gowon told his nation on becoming "supreme commander" four years ago, "the basis for unity is not there." But in the interval, the young general has himself done much to puncture that gloomy appraisal. And the Ibos now appear ready, if given the chance, to forget the war and get on with the task of nation-building. On the tenth anniversary of its independence, Nigeria is, for the second time, trying to make a go of it. And the chances look better than ever that this time it may succeed.

IV. WEST AFRICA'S ECONOMY

EDITOR'S INTRODUCTION

When they talk about West Africa, diplomats and scholars sometimes divide it into "countries" and "noncountries" or "haves" and "have-nots." The "haves" are those more fortunate nations which, by virtue of their size, location, economic resources, and political stability, may one day attain economic self-sufficiency.

In the opening selection, Tufts University Professor Robert L. West looks at both rich and poor countries, their special problems and needs. This is followed by a brief excerpt from L. Gray Cowan's book, *The Dilemmas of African Independence,* discussing African socialism. Studies of individual countries follow: a "have"—the Ivory Coast; a "may-have"—Ghana; and a "have-not, tiny Gambia, which has less than half the population of New York City. Liberia, an example of a dual or enclave economy, completes the economic profile of West Africa.

The region's economic trends and prospects are reviewed in the next selections. First is a comment on the population explosion. Economist Andrew M. Kamarck and correspondents John Lambert and Jim Hoagland follow; each assesses the outlook for increased trade and foreign investment. An article from *African Development* (London) discusses the new climate for investors. Frederic Hunter analyzes the drive toward Africanization, or economic decolonization. Finally, Ghanaian Robert K. A. Gardiner, a United Nations official, reflects on the economic lessons of the first decade.

ECONOMIC DEVELOPMENT IN PERSPECTIVE [1]

Just ten years ago John F. Kennedy, then chairman of the African Subcommittee of the Senate Foreign Relations Committee, reported to his Senate colleagues:

Africa is going through a revolution. The word is out—and spreading like wildfire in nearly a thousand languages and dialects—that it is no longer necessary to remain forever poor or forever in bondage.

In the intervening decade, the bondage of colonial dominion, at least, has largely—but not quite fully—disappeared from the continent. But the poverty of Africa is something else. It not only persists; it pervades. . . .

By such indicators as per capita income, exports and energy consumption; or the contribution of manufacturing to total output, the proportion of the population engaged in market-related activities and the share of primary products in exports; or illiteracy and mass media exposure—Africa lags behind the development status of the other continents. . . .

The poverty of Africa—the lack of adequate material and human resources which make successful development possible—contributes to a widening gap not only between Africa and the industrial countries but also between Africa and other developing areas of the world.

A target minimum growth rate of 5 per cent per annum was established for the United Nations Development Decade . . . [the sixties]. Relatively strong growth performance in the past few years, which Africa has shared with the other developing areas, has enabled the developing world as a whole to meet this target for the first eight years of the decade. But the growth rate in Africa has not kept pace. . . .

Only in the average per capita receipt of foreign aid do the countries of Africa lead other developing areas of the world, and even this lead has fallen steadily since 1961. In

[1] From "Economic Development in Africa Today," by Robert L. West, professor of development diplomacy, Fletcher School of Law and Diplomacy, Tufts University. *Current History*. 56:263-8+. My. '69. Reprinted by permission of Current History, Inc.

marked contrast to the experience of Latin America and Asia, the flow of development assistance and external private investment received by African countries reached a plateau in 1961-1962; the trend of development financing from abroad during the second half of the Development Decade is evidently downward for Africa, chiefly as a result of a sharp decline in the flow to North Africa. . . .

It is the contrasts, not the uniformities, which most impress an observer of the economic scene in Africa; there are striking contrasts between countries and within individual nations. No continuous boundary separates the most modern and technologically advanced from the traditional and primitive. The economic geography of Africa consists of a scatter of economic "islands," comprising all together less than 5 per cent of the tropical African land area, where 85 per cent of total economic output is concentrated; the "islands" are separated by vast spaces of low fertility, scattered population and primitive technology. These "islands" of concentrated economic activity encompass the coastal locations of convenient trade and transport access to the interior of the continent, the zones of mineral concentration, and the highland areas of fertile soil and reliable rainfall.

In their origin, the contrasts between the modern, progressive "islands" and the stagnating hinterland may be traceable to natural geographic factors, but they have been greatly accentuated by the colonial economic experience. [Former] World Bank President Eugene Black described the results of goals pursued during the colonial era in a lecture at the University of Georgia in 1961:

Investment in Africa has done much more to expand industry and commerce on other continents than on the African continent itself. Despite its resources, despite billions in capital, the benefits of modern economic development in Africa have not spread out very far from the mines and plantations.

From the colonial era, also, there persist basic differences of outlook, goals and methods of approach implanted by the different styles of British, French, Belgian, Portuguese and

Spanish dominion. Independence has meant different things in French- and English-speaking nations, not least with respect to the nature of residual and continuing economic association with the former metropole. On the whole, commercial, financial and administrative ties to France—despite increasing French efforts to escape some of the burdens of exclusive association—are stronger in Francophonic countries than are the links between English-speaking African nations and the United Kingdom.

Finally, to assess the setting in which economic development is pursued in Africa today, we must take into account the economic disruption in some African countries occasioned by the struggle for independence or the legacy of political conflicts inherited by the new nations. . . .

Economic Diversification

African exports are almost entirely comprised of primary commodities; most nations concentrate heavily on one or two major crops. Because of difficulties encountered in marketing these commodities abroad and because of rising world prices of products imported for domestic consumption, many African nations have embarked upon a policy of diversification of production by establishing import-substitution industries, encouraging self-sufficiency in food production, and expanding production of secondary crops demanded on the world market. Economic diversification has been among the nominal goals of nearly all African countries in the past, but only in recent years have the vicissitudes of the world market resulted in significant channeling of resources to this end. . . .

Except for the Ivory Coast, the European Economic Community Associated States of the Yaoundé Agreement—whose traditional agricultural exports have been subsidized by the EEC until recently—have not diversified to the degree of the former British colonies, where the full impact of world market forces has been felt. In Senegal, however, the reaction to the removal of the French subsidy for groundnuts has been an effort to encourage diversification into cotton and food production. It seems likely that the trend toward diversification will manifest itself in the future in Francophonic Africa as well as among the former British dependencies.

Rural Development Emphasis

African governments increasingly regard rural areas as essential contributors to the development process and essential recipients of its benefits. This tendency to emphasize rural development is partly a concomitant of the effort to diversify, but it is partly also the result of a growing recognition that the economic potential and political strength of the African peasantry were neglected or underestimated in the postindependence plans for rapid industrialization.

Africa's rural areas were often neglected in the years immediately following independence when the energies of most nations were directed toward industrialization and urban development. . . . In Ghana, the Ivory Coast and Senegal, governments seemed content to use the foreign exchange earned from the export of agricultural produce as a means of financing industrial development, with little of their expenditures going into the rural sector of the economy. Gradually, however, this neglect of the rural sector has ended as governments have become aware of the need to convince farmers to diversify crop production, to produce more food, and to engage in more self-help projects—and as farmers themselves have demanded a greater share of the fruits of economic development and greater participation in decisions affecting development. . . .

Economic Self-Reliance

In a variety of ways, African nations are adapting to the diminished prospects of foreign development assistance and investment. Substantial efforts are being made to generate more internal savings and to prepare government budgets that will terminate foreign subsidies of current expenditures. Recognizing that increased investment is largely dependent on the mobilization of financing by governments in Africa,

African states are focusing attention on means of improving their fiscal systems and on means of determining priorities in allocating government expenditures....

For some African nations there is an even more urgent pressure to reduce dependence on foreign assistance and investment. In the decade before independence and in the immediate postindependence period, a few African countries accumulated a burden of foreign indebtedness which now bears very heavily on government revenues and foreign exchange earnings. Foreign capital financed projects which have failed to produce earnings sufficient to provide for debt service and repayment. In Sierra Leone, foreign debt obligations absorbed 22 per cent of all government expenditures in the 1967-1968 fiscal year. Ghana has required a rescheduling of the debts accumulated in the last years of the regime of Kwame Nkrumah and has adopted policies to restrain government spending, to revise her tax structures, and to rationalize economic policy making to channel funds to more productive uses....

Although concrete action to increase internal financing is manifest in only a few African countries, the need to adopt such practices is widely recognized. The recent conference of African planners, convened by the United Nations Economic Commission for Africa, agreed that "African countries need to aim at achieving national self-reliance and avoid drawing up plans in which external assistance [has] a preponderant share."

Trade Cooperation

The commitment to expanded intra-African economic cooperation is not new, nor are the development problems in many African countries that make such cooperation attractive. Domestic markets in Africa are generally limited in size, and tariff barriers seriously impair the growth of African industries. There is a persisting trend toward the creation of larger intra-African free trade units with increasing attention to the means of equalizing the benefits for participating nations....

The story of African economic development today is one of poverty and a generally disappointing pace of achievement, but of wide diversity in performance and potential. The consequences of the great political changes on the continent are still working themselves out and dominate the formation of economic policies. The significant contemporary trends have in common a characteristic of adaptation to the need for greater self-reliance on national resources and on the potential gains from enlarged cooperation among the African states.

AFRICAN SOCIALISM [2]

Socialism is . . . regarded throughout the developing world as a progressive force in contrast to capitalism. It represents an ideology designed to promote the national economy for the good of the people as a whole, not for the profit of a minority. The egalitarian content of socialism in its advocacy of a common share in the national product fits closely with the nationalists' goal of equality of treatment in every sphere of life.

In their present formulation, socialist doctrines in Africa are frequently vague, incomplete, and even contradictory. There is disagreement on both the terminology and the content. Sékou Touré, for example, maintains that there is no such doctrine as African socialism; he disagrees that there can be any modification of socialist doctrine purely in terms of its application to Africa. In this stand, he is, of course, in agreement with the Soviet theorists who insist that socialism cannot be altered to fit the immediate requirements of a particular country or area. Nevertheless, current interpretations of socialism cover a wide spectrum in Africa, ranging from the more rigid, theoretical stand adopted by Touré and the Parti Démocratique de Guinée through the remarkable *tour de force* of Senghor in Senegal, which at-

[2] From *The Dilemmas of African Independence*, by L. Gray Cowan, director of the Institute of African Studies, Columbia University rev. ed. Walker. '68. p 9-10. Copyright © 1964, 1968 by Walker and Company, New York. By permission of the publisher.

tempts to combine socialism and humanism, to the broadly African *Ujamaa* of Nyerere in Tanzania.

Whatever may be its particular interpretation in the hands of the African governments, socialism has everywhere in the continent a strong pragmatic strain. In part, this derives from the awareness by African leaders of the strong inclination toward private initiative to be found everywhere in the African trading community and of the continuing necessity for most African economies to seek development capital from private external sources. Although emphasis tends to be on public ownership, in part because much of the development capital and technical skills remains in government hands, a substantial place is left in socialist planning for private ownership of industrial facilities and for the private entrepreneur.

Although many of the concepts of socialism in Africa are derived from Marxist-Leninist doctrine, as well as much of the terminology used in the African writings on socialism, a variety of strands from other sources are to be found. The thought of Rousseau, of Hobbes, and of Washington are intermixed with elements of peculiarly African thinking. African socialism categorically denies a major element of Marxist thought, the class struggle. This aspect of Marxism, it is argued, is not applicable to Africa, since traditional African society was not divided into a class structure. The class struggle, Senghor argues, was developed by Marx to apply to conditions in Europe at the period of industrialization of the early nineteenth century. It has, therefore, little relevance to African problems of the twentieth century. It is clear that one of the major goals of the contemporary leaders of Africa is to avoid dividing societies into mutually antagonistic classes as a result of the process of industrialization and modernization. Senghor insists that Africa can substitute cooperation for the class struggle and thereby free the continent from the internal social clashes that accompanied the transformation of nineteenth century European society. Although there may be some truth to the assertion that traditional African societies were not based upon class division as it is known in modern Europe, it seems highly doubtful that the modernization of the continent can be accomplished without some degree of antagonism through the presence in society of increasingly differentiated economic interest groups. Senghor adds, however, one further point of Marxist doctrine which he feels is particularly applicable to Africa today. This is the concept of work as a key to development. The creation of a modern industrial society cannot be achieved overnight or by magic and wishful thinking; it can only come through the physical labor of all members of the society. This theme is echoed in East Africa in the frequently heard phrase, *Uhuru na kazi*—Freedom and work.

IVORY COAST 1968: BOOM [3]

Abidjan: In the Ivory Coast the fact of economic boom is inescapable. You see it downtown, in the office building whose ground floor houses a replica of Le Drugstore of Paris. You see it across the bay in the glass-and-concrete rise of the Hotel Ivoire, which provides de luxe breakfasts for visiting foreign businessmen and African statesmen and de luxe bowling for Abidjan's thousands of Frenchmen.

You see it in the towers of the oil refinery. You see it in the flour mill—and in the good French bread. You see it in the steady stream of trucks bearing huge loads of logs, coffee or bananas over some of Africa's best-paved roads, which lead from upcountry plantations to the port of Abidjan.

The boom makes the Ivory Coast an exception in Africa, where pessimists have a depressing record of accurately predicting political upheaval and economic stagnation. Here even the pessimists are optimistic; they see significant problems but think the odds are at least even that the Ivory Coast will solve them.

[3] From "Bumps in Ivory Coast Boom," by Anthony Astrachan, Washington *Post* correspondent. Washington *Post*. p B 2. My. 5, '68. © The Washington Post. Reprinted by permission.

President Félix Houphouët-Boigny has made the Ivory Coast an exception in other ways....

Houphouët . . . runs one of the few African economies that give a major role to private enterprise. Its boom stands out all the more in contrast to the faltering statist economics of neighboring Guinea and Mali.

Reliance on Foreigners

He leads a country that makes no attempt to hide its reliance on foreigners. The 32,000 Frenchman (more than twice as many as at independence in 1960) run most of the economy. They hold most of the key positions in the government below cabinet level. Houphouët's motto is *"Pas d'Africanisation au rabais,"* or "No Africanization at a discount" —that is, at the expense of quality. Few African states take such an approach.

What's more, nearly 1 million of the Ivory Coast's 4.4 million population are people from other African states who have migrated for a share of the boom. Still more are members of tribes that spill across the border but whose centers of gravity are in neighboring countries.

The dimensions of the boom itself are exceptional. The Ivory Coast's gross domestic product grew by an average of 9.5 per cent a year from 1960 to 1965. It grew 8.5 per cent from $1.012 billion in 1965 to $1.098 billion in 1966. Many African countries have to struggle to achieve 4 per cent growth.

The country remains the world's third largest coffee producer, and coffee and cocoa account for 60 per cent of Ivorian exports. But diversification has probably gone further here than anywhere else in black Africa. Exports of bananas, pineapple and rubber are flourishing; domestic production of cotton and rice are zooming; when new oil-palm plantations come into production next year the economy will be even broader.

And the country is moving away from total reliance on agriculture toward a larger role for industry. One reason is that many foreign investors, including some American companies, are making the Ivory Coast their African base.

Aware of Problems

The boom, the private enterprise and the foreign help have enabled Houphouët to organize a government and a set of planners who seem more aware of the problems that need solving than most of their counterparts in Africa.

One of those problems is urbanization. Abidjan already holds 10 per cent of the country's 4.4 million people and is growing even faster than the population as a whole.

The flight from the land to the cities is found all over Africa. The Ivory Coast is trying harder than most African states to create "a harmonious balance between city and country," in the words of the 1967 Plan Law, but here too it is an uphill fight. And taking care of the growing urban population costs so much it can disrupt all economic development efforts.

Another problem is European domination of the economy. The high-rise buildings, the highway cloverleafs, the French stores, the Europeans behind executive-suite desks and store counters right down to the fish market, all make Abidjan seem a bit of an artificial transplant in the humid West African climate.

The boom the Europeans have helped create is very real, but Ivorians are already asking, "When is it going to belong to us?"

Attempts to solve the two problems are often intertwined.

President Houphouët, for instance, has forbidden top officials to build houses in the capital—a favorite form of quick-paying investment throughout Africa—until they have built one in their home towns or villages.

This can make villagers feel they don't have to move to the city to live in or among new buildings. And it can make them feel that Africans have a visible stake in the country's wealth.

Temporarily Abortive

The attempt can boomerang, however. Houphouët's home town, Yamassoukrou, is the site of many development plums not justified by its 3,000 population. One is a spread of new housing, concrete bungalows with corrugated metal roofs, that has the air of an African version of Levittown.

Running water, sewage systems and electricity have not spread as fast as the housing; that kind of investment is not so easy to solicit or implement as construction and the need is not clearly realized. Living in the new houses is a very mixed pleasure.

Half of them are unoccupied anyway, because so few people in Yamassoukrou can afford the rent or mortgage payments on a new house. The effort seems at least temporarily abortive, neither counterbalancing Abidjan's attractions nor providing real African participation in the economy.

Education can also be used to solve both the problems of urbanization and European domination. Spreading it into the bush can make village life more compelling; training people is necessary before they can run things as well as the Europeans do.

But in Abidjan, 82 per cent of school-age children are in school; in the back bush, the figure is only 4 per cent. And since the Ivory Coast spends 25 per cent of its budget on education, with a primary-school graduate costing the government $3,000 and a high school graduate $14,000, it is easier to concentrate that kind of investment in the cities to reduce unit costs.

A different kind of training is provided by the Service Civique, modeled on Israeli patterns and directed by Israelis. The Service runs ten camps where peasant boys learn to read and write and to use modern farming methods. Some go on to a training school for instructors at Bouake, but 3,000 have gone back to their villages in batches from 12 to 20.

The Israelis say the Service Civique graduates earn four to five times as much as untrained peasants in the same village (something like $100 a year instead of $40 a year).

This kind of result means more people on the land, as African producers, meeting the problems of urbanization and foreign domination.

Vocational Training

Another double-barreled effort is vocational training centers scattered around the country. Ivorian mechanics, carpenters, masons and other skilled workers are needed to take over from Europeans or "foreign" Africans. It is significant that European companies make fewer efforts to train Ivorians themselves than they do in some other African countries.

And the attitudes of many of the Europeans frustrate the kind of change that efforts like vocational training are supposed to make. They are often not interested in expansion if it means more work for them, in service that builds profits, in efforts toward African fulfillment.

Attempts to solve one problem do not always help solve the other. The Ivory Coast is planning a $95 million dam on the Bandama River, with U.S. and Italian loans, and a $28 million port at San Pedro that will create thousands of jobs and open up the very wild west of the country. Both provide attractions to compete with Abidjan, but both will depend on foreign money and technicians.

Many analysts think the foreign investment is more important, for good or for bad, than personnel. But European personnel can continue to dominate enterprises in which Ivorian agencies have taken a piece of the stock and to run things so that their payoff takes priority over Ivorian needs.

The regime must pull off the trick of maintaining the boom while simultaneously Africanizing it fast enough to avoid upheaval.

The odds are better here than anyplace else in Africa where the problem exists, but no veteran thinks it's a sure bet. And European domination is the kind of problem that could impel the generation that follows Houphouët to make drastic changes.

IVORY COAST 1970: BOOM'S END? [4]

President Félix Houphouët-Boigny of the Ivory Coast seems intent on keeping his promises.

Following his much-heralded "dialogue," a series of twenty-two meetings with various groups throughout the country, President Houphouët-Boigny has initiated important policy changes and brought new talent into his Cabinet.

In a special communiqué, he announced a Cabinet reshuffle, the reassignment of local administrators (prefects) to new posts, salary increases in both private and public sectors, the release of funds for agricultural training camps, subsidies for the Ivorian Transporters Union, and plans for a presidential tour of the eighteen prefectures in which "working visits" would focus on the role of local officials.

All of these measures are direct results of complaints raised by Ivorians during the "dialogue" sessions, which ran from October to December [1969].

Cabinet Reshuffled

To implement these decisions with the right mixture of "political militancy" and youth, the president dismissed five members of his Cabinet while announcing eleven new ministerial appointments. The Cabinet, whose 22 members include 18 university graduates, is intended to give the government a new look and a new spirit in its tenth year.

While advertising itself as "West Africa's most prosperous country," the Ivory Coast has experienced serious economic and political problems in the past year.

It has paid for its healthy balance of payments and an increasing rate of economic growth with low salaries and a high cost of living.

Also there is mass unemployment of Ivorians while trained expatriates run the economy, and a lack of social services.

It became dramatically clear to the president during his "dialogue" that these problems could cause serious political unrest. Suggestions for changes in the single party, the Parti Démocratique de Côte d'Ivoire, and even primary elections at regional level were direct challenges to the position of the president and the regime.

Unrest Widespread

Local problems also had become threatening to the government. The refusal of the army to put down a local demonstration protesting market taxes and the location of a new market undermined the power of the prefect in Daloa, a western town.

Renewed activity by the Agni secessionist movement in the southeastern area of Aboisso led to military intervention and the death of two Agni tribesmen. These disturbances came after labor demonstrations in the capital, Abidjan, during the fall and the mass arrest of some 1,600 unemployed young men.

The government's forceful response to local problems caused much resentment and probably forced the president to deny that there were any political prisoners in the country.

Local Structures Added

Political and economic problems, therefore, seemed to demand executive action if stability was to be maintained. With this in mind, the president's December 31 communiqué provided some direct solutions and suggested others. At the top, ministers in charge of allocation of opportunities, such as education, labor, social affairs, civil service, and construction and town planning, were all sacked. In their place, young highly trained civil servants were appointed to renovate departments and carry out new programs.

At the local level, the six prefects were rotated to new positions and twelve new prefectures set up "to bring administrators closer to the administered."

Daloa received a capable, well-liked administrator from the north and Aboisso found itself administered by a strong, experienced prefect.

Special groups also received good news. The transporters would receive more money for the movement of commercial coffee and cocoa. The tenants, who had demanded more low-cost housing, were told of the release of new credit for that purpose. And the teachers were told that their profession was "the priority of priorities" in the Ivory Coast.

These measures are designed to continue present political stability. . . . Their failure, and consequent public discontent, would be persuasive reasons for him [the president] to step down, following the example of General Charles de Gaulle, a man he much admires.

More important, stepping down would remove him from the precarious position of all African leaders during times of political unrest. This action, however, would leave a political vacuum at the top, leading perhaps to political conflict. This would destroy his carefully nurtured climate for foreign investment.

While in a difficult position, the president is well known for his political skill. Observers here are left with a final question: Will this be enough?

GHANA: HELP WANTED [5]

Dr. Kofi Busia's first task as Ghana's new premier was to tour the capitals of the West begging for money. He had to

[5] Editorial, "Ghana Deserves a Square Deal—European Companies share Debts Guilt." *African Development* (London). p 3. N. '69. Reprinted by permission.

go cap in hand pleading for cash to pay off the debts of his archopponent, Kwame Nkrumah. This alone, together with his promises of sound financial management should be argument enough to make his creditors generous. But there is far more to say.

Firstly, it is not only Nkrumah who is to blame. Many British and European firms are guilty of allowing Ghana to run up debts for foolhardy schemes. They seized their short-term profits, knowing full well that the repayment problems were piling up.

Second, if the West wants to enjoy healthy trading relations with black Africa's wealthiest nation (per capita), then it is in her interests to see Ghana restored to prosperity in the shortest possible period.

Third (and most important of all), the West should recognize that a point of principle is at stake. It is the question of whether or not it is prepared to give Western parliamentary democracy a fresh start in Africa.

For three years the Ghana military government tried every possible means to keep the economy going while honoring its debt obligations. The growth rate was reduced to below 1 per cent, 70,000 out of a labor force of 345,000 were kept unemployed by the squeeze. A historic balance of trade and payments deficit was turned into a surplus. And IMF [International Monetary Fund] instructions were carried out to the letter.

For three years the Ghana people have made heroic economic efforts without enjoying the fruits of their labors. All Busia is now asking is that they should be granted a small increase in their standard of living while the economy gains strength.

To deny him this will almost certainly lead to trouble, to the fall of a democratic regime and to the final repudiation of the debts. Britain's miserable £1 million of tied aid will not go very far, in the light of the £500 million which Ghana owes. Nor is it much compared with the £20 million that Kenya has received, mainly to compensate white farmers.

As Dr. Busia told the UN last month:

National development in Ghana has been virtually at a standstill for five years now. . . . I hope our creditors, who have shown a willingness earlier on to recognize the need for dealing with this debt problem through negotiation and concerted action, will be equally willing to listen to the aspirations of our people, and cooperate in arrangements for debt repayment which will make it possible for our new government to respond to their needs.

GAMBIA: A "HAVE-NOT" MAKES DO [6]

Gambia, jabbing like a long thorn into the side of Senegal, has 350,000 inhabitants spread over an area the size of Los Angeles County. Its national airline is a ticket office and its one shoe store is usually out of shoelaces.

The annual budget of $8 million, less than that of a middling business company, won't accommodate a mission to the United Nations.

But Gambia, independent since February 1965, and thriving on a minor scale, is not about to stop being a country. Just three months ago it became a republic, dropping Queen Elizabeth II as head of state.

Outspoken Gambians, and quiet ones when asked, say they want no part of political union with their African neighbor. Prices are lower and life is easier in this former English colony where teacups clink and cricket bats thud.

Most African rulers travel behind motorcycles and automatic weapons, but President Dauda K. Jawara does his own shopping alone.

Gambian immigration officials make sure that visitors find a taxi from the airport. The political opposition can grumble at will. And after all, Gambians say, why waste money on a UN mission?

[6]Associated Press release: "Gambia: Independent, Thriving—in Small Way." Text from *Christian Science Monitor*. p 5. Jl. 27, '70. Reprinted by permission of Associated Press Newsfeatures.

Bathurst, a grubby town of 30,000 founded by the British in 1819 to use in chasing slavers, rocks from November to April when the tourists come.

Peanuts, tourists, and smuggling are about Gambia's only riches. One official source in Senegal has estimated that $5 million is lost annually to Senegalese coffers from two-way smuggling.

The Senegalese finance minister, Jean Colin, a former French accountant, made an attack eighteen months ago on "unrecorded reexports." Nationalism surged in Gambia and each country flashed fangs.

It's quieter now, but Senegal is trying to watch the four-hundred-mile border laced with creeks and open bush tracks.

At one point, every Gambian man, woman, and child would have had to smoke three packs a day to consume all the cigarettes imported. When Senegal's peanut farmers have a bad crop, Gambia, where prices are higher and in cash, has a mysteriously good one.

Well-tuned business sources estimate smuggling is down, although it is still rampant in favorite items like transistor radios and textiles.

Senegal's breadbasket is a rich strip in the south called the Casamance, and the only feasible way to get there is on the main highway straight through Gambia.

A Senegambian secretariat was set up in 1968 to seek means of drawing together. It is to oversee a United Nations survey of the Gambia River Basin and a British study of the land around it for use by both countries.

President Jawara and Senegalese President Léopold Sédar Senghor get together at least once a year. "Senegal will come to our help if we are ever threatened by attack," a key Gambian official said, adding with a grin: "But that's highly unlikely since we are almost entirely surrounded by Senegal."

Gambia has no army, and has had no major disturbance here since a slave revolt in the early 1600s.

LIBERIA'S "DUAL" ECONOMY [7]

Liberia is the fifth smallest country in Africa with a population of about 1 million persons, an area of 43,000 square miles, and a density of twenty-three persons a square mile. Some of its economic, political and social features are not shared by other African countries because Liberia was never a colony of a European power. It became an independent republic in 1847 at the initiative of a small colony of several thousand free Negroes from the United States (Americo-Liberians) who claimed sovereignty over a hinterland of some twenty tribal groups. For the most part, tribal persons were little affected by European commerce and culture until well into the twentieth century.

The salient characteristics of Liberian economy are the recent start of private and governmental development activities, the unusual extent to which new lines of production are undertaken by foreign firms, the extreme concentration of activities in primary production for export (rubber and iron ore), and the relative absence of systematic national planning to transform traditional sectors of the economy and initiate other structural changes. In short, Liberia is a prime example of a "dual" economy and an "enclave" economy. It has one of the highest rates of output growth on record because of heavy European and American investments in iron-ore mining and rubber, but remains largely undeveloped otherwise....

Despite its historical association with the United States, its rich resource base relative to population, and generous external assistance by foreign governments and international agencies, Liberia must be placed among the least developed countries in Africa. In 1962, less than 10 per cent of the population was literate, the quality of its educational establishment was low, the traditional divisions between tribal

[7] From *The Economies of Africa*, by Peter Robson and D. A. Lury, eds. Northwestern University Press. Evanston, Ill. '69. p 287, 314-15. © George Allen and Unwin Ltd., 1969. Reprinted by permission. Peter Robson is professor of economics at the University of St. Andrews; D. A. Lury, senior lecturer at the University of Kent at Canterbury.

Liberians and the Americo-Liberian descendants of the colonial settlers remained in force, and traditional governmental procedures and preferences had not been appreciably
revised to serve development needs.

The great burgeoning of rubber and iron-ore production
by foreigners since 1950 has had relatively little developmental impact: the unskilled labor force working for wages
has almost tripled, but the enlarged receipt of money wages
has not induced appreciably more production for the domestic market; rather it has increased the effective demand
for imported consumption goods. The enlarged governmental revenues (which increased eightfold between 1950 and
1960) and enlarged borrowing from abroad—both of which
are direct consequences of the rapid growth in primary
products for export—for the most part have not been spent
in ways which increase the productive capacity of the nation.
Most professionally trained Liberians worked for the government. The uneducated mass of tribal Liberians grew
subsistence and traditional cash crops and worked as unskilled laborers on rubber farms. A few had acquired vocational and clerical skills. Only in rubber production has
there been marked growth in an economic activity undertaken by Liberians.

In 1962 there was nothing that could reasonably be called
developmental planning. Neither effective plan nor personnel existed. Liberia's principal tasks in research and in developmental planning are to transform subsistence agriculture (and especially to increase production of marketed rice,
and its protein staple, fish), to reform its educational establishment to supply the growing demand for skilled and professional labor, and to undertake feasibility studies for new
lines of processing and manufacture. Its most tenacious problems are institutional and require policies to reform traditional social and political organizations: to abolish forced
recruitment of labor, to reform traditional land tenure arrangements, to reform the traditional administration of the
tribal hinterland in ways which provide incentives for tribal

persons to enlarge their production for sale, and to allow them access to higher education and political expression.

LIBERIAN PRIORITIES [8]

Since the early 1950s, when iron-ore extraction began, Liberia's GNP [gross national product] has increased at rates varying from 4 to 10 per cent per year. At the same time, population has grown at only about 2 per cent per year. The overall growth rate therefore has been favorable. However, there have been major problems in distributing the benefits to the population as a whole. Among these are the following:

Income from large-scale iron-ore and rubber industries which account for about 42 per cent of the country's GNP is controlled by a limited number of owners and stockholders.

Employment opportunities are limited by a lag in the growth of manufacturing and service industries.

Agricultural production is seriously restricted by poor soils, adverse climatic conditions, lagging technology, and inadequately trained manpower.

High debt service, resulting from overoptimistic projections of future iron-ore and rubber earnings during the 1950s, has been a serious problem during much of the past decade and claims some 20 per cent of government revenue.

These conditions continue to limit the pace of diffused economic and social growth in Liberia. Aggregate growth declined in 1969 and will probably remain comparatively low in 1970 due to a tapering off of major new investments, such as iron-ore-pelletizing facilities; water, sewerage and power systems; and school and hospital construction. However, potential investments in timber and wood-products industries, and oil and other mineral exploration may provide

[8] From *U.S. Foreign Aid in Africa: Proposed Fiscal Year 1971 Program.* United States. Agency for International Development. Washington, D.C. 20523. '70. p 49-51.

a needed stimulus. U.S. private investment in Liberia through 1968 totaled $174 million.

Despite these problems, the Government of Liberia has honored its international financial commitments, improved its budget and fiscal policies and procedures over the past several years and steadily expanded government revenue, largely through improved tax enforcement and other revenue programs. Problems affecting agriculture, education, health and public infrastructure have been attacked and some progress made. Efforts to attract additional foreign investment while expanding Liberian entrepreneurship and employment are receiving increased attention.

Complementing the above and other positive governmental steps toward development, Liberia has maintained a free market economy and supported regional cooperation. At the same time, it remains essentially free of civil disorder. Mineral and forest reserves and an expanding supply of trained manpower provide an adequate base for sustained growth at a reasonable rate during the next decade. . . .

Education: Liberia's most serious problems in the field of education are at the junior and senior secondary levels. Improvements are necessary since this level provides terminal education for middle-level skills and preparation for higher education. . . . At the postsecondary level, Liberia has a relatively large number of degree holders as a result of foreign scholarship programs over the years and its two institutions of higher learning, both of which have received AID [Agency for International Development] and other assistance.

Health Care: Liberia lacks basic preventive and curative facilities and programs and has only one doctor per 13,000 people. . . .

Agriculture: Agriculture provides employment for two thirds of Liberia's population. Continued low levels of food production have necessitated increased food imports, particularly food grains, and serious problems result from poor soil, adverse climate and lack of modern technology and investment resources.

POPULATION EXPLOSION [9]

No continent except Latin America witnessed such a startling population boom in the sixties as Africa. From 273 million in 1960, Africa's human total soared to an estimated 330 million in 1968. But the figures are notoriously inaccurate and it may be that the continent is much closer to the 400 million mark than it believes. According to the International Planned Parenthood Federation: "For some African countries, the statistics are not up to date and are only estimates. Where a recent census has been held, the figures often show an alarming increase over the previous official guess."

Experts believe that Africa's population will be, give or take a few millions here or there, beyond 450 million by 1980—an addition of almost 200 million on to the total at the start of this decade.

The administrative, educational and economic difficulties such growth creates are clear enough. Yet many African leaders argue forcefully that they do not need to worry about birth control for a long time. They say they must reach an optimum level of population before economic take-off can be launched. Many African nations can muster no more people than would fit into some Indian city such as Bombay. Indeed, India alone dwarfs all Africa in numbers, despite the vast difference in area.

Looked at in another way, Africa has 21 people per square kilometer of agricultural land, whereas Asia has 147

[9] Excerpt: Population: Astonishing Population Explosion Lies Ahead, from "Africa in the Seventies." *African Development* (London). p 11. Ja. '70. Reprinted by permission.

and Europe 52. However, these comparisons are not meaningful unless the productivity of labor is considered. On this basis, Africa fares badly and the continent will be confronted with acute economic penalties unless the land can be made to supply more and will have to expend vital foreign currency on feeding more and more tireless reproducers.

Modern medicine has helped to transform the scene, cropping the death rate, virtually eliminating endemic diseases such as malaria and now offering possible remedies for the most intractable of all African woes, the enfeebling bilharzia [also known as the schistosome or blood fluke, which causes a severe tropical disease—Ed.]. On the other side, there has been hostility to outside help in limiting the surge of population. In the Francophone countries, nothing is being done, but the need has been recognized in Ghana, Nigeria and Kenya; family-planning experts are active in all three places. On the Indian Ocean island of Mauritius, birth control is being urgently promoted as the only hope of saving the economy from disaster.

However, the issue has strong racial overtones. The argument can be put forward that by promoting family planning, the developed countries are trying to guarantee their own survival. By 1980, Europe will have little more than a tenth of the world's population and be little ahead of Africa.

The population expansion brings in its train the difficulty of finding jobs for the many thousands of young people coming on to the labor markets. Industrial development has proved that it can only absorb a tiny part of this new generation. Some African governments are taking steps to tackle the dilemma—but in the end there is only one way: this is to turn the people's faces away from the towns to the rural areas.

It is reasonable to forecast that this will be the most testing problem of the seventies in social terms for Africa's leaders. Within it there is political dynamite.

NEEDED: LARGER MARKETS [10]

Practically all economic analysis of development problems in Africa comes out with the conclusion that a necessary condition for faster industrial growth in most countries is a larger size of market and that the small economic size of most African countries is a severe handicap to establishing industry. The initial impact of independence was to destroy most of the existing larger economic units, such as the federations in West Africa and the monetary unions under the West African and East African Currency Boards. . . .

In West Africa, Dahomey, Ivory Coast, Mauritania, Togo, Senegal, and Upper Volta remain in a multinational currency union, and the four Equatorial states and Cameroon form another. Various other initiatives—for example the Union Douanière et Economique de l'Afrique de l'Ouest, consisting of Mauritania, Senegal, Mali, Niger, Upper Volta, Ivory Coast and Dahomey—are still mostly at the beginning stage or even the declaration of intention or planning stage.

Aside from the political will to set them up and make them work, economic unions, common markets, or customs unions need to have as a base a better inter-African infrastructure. . . . A step in this direction has been taken in recent years with the creation of a working group consisting of the African Development Bank, the Economic Commission for Africa, the United Nations Development Program, and the World Bank to plan improvements in the inter-African network of transport, telecommunications, and power. One concrete result of this joint planning has been the decision to construct power lines from Ghana to Togo and Dahomey by which the Volta Project in Ghana will provide electricity to the other two countries. There is also some progress being made in beginning the improvement of roads between countries. . . .

[10] From "African Economic Development: Problems and Prospects," by Andrew M. Kamarck, economist, former head of the World Bank's Africa section. *Africa Report.* 14:18-20. Ja. '69. Reprinted by permission from Africa Report Magazine.

Over the next ten years, world technological progress is likely to make possible a big step forward in bringing African countries into closer communication with each other. The jet airplane in its "jumbo" phase should reduce air transport costs considerably and may well make air transport much more economic in large parts of Africa than the road or rail alternatives. For a continent with large empty spaces separating centers of development, air transport is peculiarly well suited since it eliminates the need for large expenditures of funds to build roads or rails traversing long distances over empty land where little traffic is generated. Communications by satellite should also be peculiarly suited to Africa because of the savings on laying wire or building microwave towers over vast distances with little intermediate traffic. Indeed, it may be more economic to use these most modern means of transport and communications in Africa than in many of the presently developed countries, which have existing large investments in transport and communication networks.

While an improved inter-African infrastructure and economic unions are important steps toward African economic development, even after they are created progress is bound to be slow since the self-reinforcing character of poverty will still continue. The creation of some additional industry may become possible when two African countries combine their markets, but the fact that there is a market of 10 million people instead of two single markets of, say, 5 million people each, is still not going to result in explosive industrialization if the 10 million have average per capita incomes of $100 or under and still have to spend the bulk of their incomes on simple food and shelter. The market for manufactures is highly income-elastic; it is only as people's incomes go up into higher levels that their demand for manufactures increases rapidly. This reinforces the gains that can come from a slower rate of population increase: one man having an income of $200 a year represents a total larger market for manufactures than that of four men, each of whom has an income of $50 a year.

The African Development Bank created in 1966 is an important advance, but it has been severely hampered by lack of funds and lack of staff. . . .

Finally, it should be mentioned that the United Nations regional agency for Africa, the Economic Commission for Africa, has during the last ten years built up an effective organization and one which is making an increasingly valuable contribution to the area.

The most important economic tie African countries have outside the region is that of the eighteen African associate members with the European Common Market. This association began in 1957, was extended in 1964 for a period of five years expiring May 31, 1969, and is now being negotiated for renewal. [It was renewed in July 1969.—Ed.]

COMMON MARKET AND THE EIGHTEEN [11]

In Luxembourg, the Common Market (EEC) and its eighteen African "Associates" recently initialed an agreement renewing for a third five-year period their trade and aid linkup.

But for the Africans the event probably had a bitter taste.

Although the association is well established as one of the most successful aid formulas yet devised, the Europeans have lost their enthusiasm and hardly bother to hide the fact.

The agreement was reached nearly a month after the second convention ran out and the session had to go until the middle of the night. The feeble imitation of the Six's old-time "marathons" was not because of any tough negotiating between the Europeans and their partners.

It was because the members did not work out their position until far too late, and then saved their own infighting

[11] Article, "African States Grumble Over EEC Trade Pact," by John Lambert, staff correspondent. *Christian Science Monitor.* p 10. Jl. 9, '69. Reprinted by permission from *The Christian Science Monitor.* © 1969 The Christian Science Publishing Society. All rights reserved.

about who was going to share what part of the bill until the last day while the Africans were kept waiting.

The new grant to the European Development Fund is pegged at $900 million which, with a further $100 million given through the European Investment Bank (the one normally used for projects within the community), makes a total of $1 billion. It seems a lot and it is 25 per cent more, in figures, than the $800 million given over the last five years.

But the Africans had asked for $1.5 billion; and there are many reasons why the new grant represents what the African countries' spokesman politely called "stagnation" for the association.

Take population: For the period 1960-67, the Six's rose 9 per cent, the eighteen's rose 15 per cent. [The Common Market, or the Six, is composed of France, Italy, West Germany, Belgium, the Netherlands, and Luxembourg.—Ed.]

Take GNP: The Community's increased 90 per cent over the same period (and its per capita income 75 per cent), whereas the GNP of the most prosperous of the eighteen, the Ivory Coast, rose only 60 per cent and its per capita income 40 per cent.

Project Costs Rise

It is not a secret that the terms of trade continue to run against the Africans. The purchasing power of a kilo of groundnuts has hardly risen since 1958, whereas the industrial products Africa needs are continually dearer.

Finally, the cost of the actual projects the fund will finance has risen, since some two thirds of the cost of any one of them is spent with European firms.

For the Africans, another disappointing aspect of the new agreement is its duration. Since the negotiations were delayed, the convention (which will be signed in Yaoundé, Cameroon, in late July) cannot be ratified and take effect for perhaps a year. That means no payments can be made in the meantime from the new fund.

If it remained a five-year convention and started a year late, the Africans would get the same sum spread over six years, not five. This would bring the annual rate down almost to what it has been hitherto.

The Europeans never raised the point, and the Africans, waiting until the Six had finished its bargaining on the total, brought it up in the closing stages.

Starting Date Negotiated

At first the Six refused an earlier date for the expiration of the new convention. Then they "negotiated," agreeing it should end five years and seven months from May 1969 (the extra month being to allow the Dutch to put a slice of the bill on their 1975 budget).

On the trade side of the association the Africans have little to be happy about either. Mainly under Dutch pressure for an "open community" and against the preference area, the Six has again cut its duties to other nonmember countries on some tropical goods.

It was not forthcoming on openings for the processed-food industries which are one of the best industrialization chances for its partners. United States pressure to end the "reverse preferences" which the African countries give the Six—as against other industrialized countries—was transmitted to the negotiating table.

In short, the same horse-trading attitude, the same lack of political vision, the same lassitude and disenchantment that mark the internal affairs of the European Community spread over the last few months to the talks with the Six's partners.

The contrast with the African negotiators, hard working, and seeing the association in political terms rather than as just a hand-out, could hardly have been greater.

NEW CLIMATE FOR INVESTORS [12]

There has been a radical change in Africa's attitude towards foreign investment during the sixties. At the beginning of the decade, in the days of militant Nkrumahism, private capital was officially despised, though privately condoned. African politicians who ruled the roost, in the days before the coups and corruption, inveighed against the whole capitalist system as a method of neocolonialist exploitation.

But, in fact, the capitalists never had it so good. The African governments simply did not have the time, or the skill to translate their blanket political condemnation into practical legislation. Thus in the early sixties the private investors rolled into Africa and the Ivory Coast and Nigeria particularly enjoyed their boom years between 1961 and 1965.

By the middle sixties European capital had nibbled at the most lucrative investment opportunities. Kenya, Nigeria, Ivory Coast, Uganda and even the Cameroons and Ghana were well on the way to establishing a widely based secondary industry. But expansion was limited because the local markets were simply not big enough to allow much more expansion. Rationalization of customs barriers and exchange rates, particularly between French- and English-speaking Africa, lagged far behind. So the Kenya biscuit maker soon found that he could supply all of his local market.

Thus in the second half of the sixties investment in secondary industry started to cool. At the same time African governments became increasingly aware of the need for further investment in heavier and more technological industry.

Chief [Obafemi] Awolowo speaking in January 1969 of the future of the Nigeria economy after the war said that the time had been reached when the country should aim at establishing heavy industries such as iron and steel, fer-

[12] From excerpt: Investment: New Climate, New Partnership, in "Africa in the Seventies." *African Development* (London). p 11-12. Ja. '70. Reprinted by permission.

tilizers, chemicals, petrochemicals and a wide range of capital goods. . . .

Meanwhile in the second half of the sixties young economists and planners were moving into the key jobs and replacing the old-style politicians. They brought a new understanding and critical attitude.

By the end of the decade a wave of realism was sweeping the continent. The wicked world of foreign capital was recognized for what it was. Foreign investors were obviously wanting a good profit out of Africa, but they were nevertheless considered invaluable in the development of the continent.

This new realism first really surfaced at the UN Amsterdam Conference in February 1969 when the top magnates of commerce confronted the leaders of the developing world. At this conference both sides recognized the value of foreign investment. The question was not, is it acceptable, but, on what conditions is it acceptable?

This attitude was reechoed at the Business International meeting at Addis Ababa in November. . . . The African countries then endorsed it by the welcome they gave to the idea of the recently proposed International Development Finance Company for Africa. In the seventies this body should bring a fresh source of private funds to a thirsty continent.

Meanwhile the African governments have been taking a closer look at the methods of control. [The year] 1969 saw the fashion in nationalizations and partial nationalizations covering such industries as . . . Sierra Leone diamonds. . . .

Partnership will obviously be the pattern for the seventies, not just in mines and oil, but throughout foreign-owned enterprise.

While international public aid is flagging, private investment in the world is growing and Africa seems certain to get its share in the seventies. The Japanese and the Americans have tasted the continent's mineral wealth; in the next ten years their industrialists will assuredly follow.

Lastly there is even the hope that the decade will see a widening of Africa's markets rather than the growing nationalism and xenophobia that has been the pattern for the sixties. If Britain joins the Common Market a start could be made in sorting out the tangle of tariffs, exchange rates, subventions and commodity agreements. This would make Africa a far more attractive market than it is today.

U.S. BUSINESS EYES AFRICA [13]

American business interests in Africa, which expanded rapidly over the past decade, are likely to swing upward even more sharply in the 1970s.

This is the view of some foreign economic analysts in Africa, who feel this way despite their recognition that much of the continent is still forming its economic and political bases.

There are indications that a decade of independence has begun to give Africa enough economic pragmatism, and enough of a growing business class of its own people, to insulate national economies to some extent from political instability.

In the past, the structures left behind by the colonialists have been so fragile that political and economic crises have gone hand in hand for most of Africa. Countries like the Congo and Ghana have been strangled economically during time of political upheaval.

Now, it appears that many Africans have had their fill of independence rhetoric and celebration, and want to get on with business.

If this trend continues, it will probably encourage an increase in American direct investment in Africa, which is now estimated to total more than $2.5 billion, a figure that is nearly triple what it was in 1960.

[13] From "Africa Ripe for Investment," by Jim Hoagland, staff correspondent. Washington *Post*. p E 1+. Ja. 18, '70. © The Washington Post. Reprinted by permission.

However, U.S. businessmen face increased competition in investment and trade in Africa, especially from the Japanese and West Germans. . . .

The old boys of the continent—Britain and France—are fairly well standing pat, with their total investment increasing only about 10 to 12 per cent in 1968 over 1967. In total investment, recent statistics show, West Germany now outranks both Britain and France in Africa, and Japan, which moved ahead of Britain in 1968, is now just behind France.

No country's economy is, of course, unaffected by major political agitation, and the African business class is still embryonic. Africa is still the preserve of the adventurous investor.

But looking at the events of 1969 that cast their shadow across the next decade, it can be theorized that none of these events turned out as badly for business as they could have, or as they were expected to.

Responding to Challenge

From an investment standpoint, businessmen can take heart from the way some of the major African countries responded to challenge, although the view is not as bright from marketing and other trade aspects. . . . [For example, there is Nigeria.]

Despite the agony of the just-ended civil war against Biafra, Nigeria's economy remains one of the healthiest in black Africa. Its agricultural exports continue to climb and tough import restrictions have fostered an internal boom for locally made consumer goods.

Nigerian planners see good prospects for attracting industrial investment in the war's wake if they can shelve the profit-remittance restrictions that have discouraged many investors from moving into Africa's largest national market.

The real key to Nigeria's economic hopes is oil. Biafran attacks seriously crippled production in 1969, but development of new fields away from insecure areas . . . rekindled oilmen's hopes for the future. Gulf, which has most of its installations off shore, seems to be in the best position for short-term profits. . . .

Other countries buffeted by change include . . . Ghana, which held an orderly election in which foreign business influence—once a favorite whipping boy of Kwame Nkrumah —was hardly mentioned. . . .

The trade picture is not as bright, either from the American or African standpoint. While not harming investment prospects thus far, . . . Nigeria's import restrictions have limited American prospects in what . . . [was] formerly . . . [one] of the best markets in Africa. . . .

From the African standpoint, the terms of trade continue to worsen. They may sell more to developed countries but they have to pay more for what they have to buy.

Experts are doubtful that the 7 to 8 per cent range of increase the United States has established over the past few years in exports to Africa will be maintained. Germany, Japan and Italy are likely to get a larger share as they increase their efforts in Africa.

AFRICANIZATION [14]

Africans are taking the jobs of non-Africans; citizens are replacing expatriates. The Africanization process represents the economic decolonization of those countries politically decolonized—that is, given independence—within the past decade.

Politically, Africa's newly emerging states have gone their own ways. They are the rulers of their own houses although in some cases lack of resources and dependence on former colonial masters limit the options they may exercise.

[14] From " 'Africanization': High Goal or Pitfall?" by Frederic Hunter, staff correspondent. *Christian Science Monitor.* p 9. O. 18, '69. Excerpted by permission from *The Christian Science Monitor.* © 1969 The Christian Science Publishing Society. All rights reserved.

Economically they have yet to achieve total independence. . . .

By and large the Africanization process is occurring in three phases. First, citizens of the new state enter the civil service, taking over jobs formerly held by colonial administrators.

In most new nations this phase of the process is well advanced. Most Europeans have been withdrawn from decision- and policy-making positions. But a new group of expatriates, the technical advisers, has arisen. It provides the technical expertise which Africans do not yet possess because of training lags.

Due to the nature of bureaucracy, to the fact that much of its work is routine requiring little initiative or originality, this is probably the easiest phase of Africanization. It is also an important adjunct to achieving political independence.

The second phase attempts to Africanize a country's commercial sector. As they enter this phase the African countries encounter myriad problems. Two alone illustrate the difficulties.

Most Africans are not equipped to go into business for themselves. To do this they must comprehend a money economy. They must read and write. Truly to succeed, they must have some knowledge and understanding of bookkeeping. It may be necessary—or at least helpful—to possess some technical skill.

But even these qualifications may not suffice if the individual has little access to capital (and loans are not easy to get) or few of the family and ethnic connections which play important roles in emerging states.

Many countries face an additional problem: Traditional societies stress communal ties rather than individuality and group relations rather than personal initiative. Even where initiative and business success exist, relatives may make demands for money, food, lodging, and school fees, depriving the successful entrepreneur of the rewards of his work.

Hostility Risked

If he refuses the demands made upon him, he risks the hostility of the group with which he primarily identifies. In other words he may become expatriated within his own country.

Senegal illustrates another aspect of the qualifications problem. There men possessing the needed educational skills aim for safe, prestigious, remunerative government jobs even though civil-service ranks now are virtually filled with men far from retirement.

Many Senegalese students nearing graduation are wary of the uncertainty and risks of business. They do not see themselves in commercial roles. These factors have caused unrest over conditions that observers say will change only when Senegalese students realize their future lies in Africanizing further the economy's commercial sector.

A second problem involves the apparent stranglehold of noncitizen groups over certain economic sectors, particularly retail trade. These groups include the Lebanese of West Africa. . . .

Some of these peoples are being forced from long-held jobs or lifetime businesses. In Ghana Lebanese are being excluded from transport and retail trade. Marginal businesses are being forced to close. Proprietors must give evidence of certain levels of business activity to continue. . . .

While these measures may seem arbitrary, resentment against these expatriate groups runs deep. For example, in Ghana many suspect Lebanese of engaging in illegal activities behind the facade of small businesses. . . .

The third phase of Africanization is in the industrial and big-business sectors.

In a truly effective way this phase has barely begun in most new African states. For instance, only seven of Kenya's top company directors are Kenyans. Of these only four are Africans.

Some countries have nationalized some industries; "puppet" managers have also been installed.

Often African countries have welcomed expatriate new-comers who offer new skills, new capital, and the probability of creating employment opportunities for Africans. But even these offers are carefully weighed. Some countries have re-jected them when they appeared to require too high a pro-portion of expatriate personnel.

Personnel Policy Described

Ghana's Volta Aluminum Company, Ltd. (Valco), a subsidiary of Kaiser Aluminum & Chemical Corporation, is an example of a high degree of Africanization in industry. The company was conceived as an integral part of the Volta Dam project because the electricity needed for its alumina smelter made the dam economically feasible. Of the present supervisory staff numbering about 260, half are expatriates. Valco expects to cut the figure to about 60 by the end of 1970.

The company uses three wage scales to pay its super-visory staff: one for Americans, one for Europeans, one for Ghanaians. The scales are based on earning capacities of a supervisor in his home country. In addition, expatriates re-ceive company housing which tends to isolate them from daily social contact with Ghanaians.

The reaction of Ghanaian supervisors to these arrange-ments is one of intellectual understanding and of emotional resentment, observers say.

Valco is, in fact, a Western industrial operation trans-planted into an African setting. Thus Africanizing the su-pervisory staff also requires training Ghanaians to think like Western industrial managers. It involves cross-cultural prob-lems and has caused some observers to question whether economic betterment is worth the price of social dislocation.

Growth Balance Sought

An even greater problem looms for those nations starting to Africanize their industrial and big-business sectors. It is that of balancing fast economic growth with a fair distribu-tion of wealth. It is a necessity to use as well as possible trained manpower and available capital without producing a small managerial elite or an alliance of government capital with expatriate technicians.

Economist Peter Marris foresees dire results should such a managerial elite, pushing for maximum economic growth, take control. He says there would be a convergence of commercial, industrial, and political power on one level, the appearance at another of vast slums and large numbers of marginal landless laborers living at the barest subsistence level.

A decade of this and "the national economy will be making encouraging progress, but the nation will be falling apart," he says.

Thus Africanization must do more than merely replace noncitizen units of manpower with citizen units. More important, the process must revolutionize a country's entire economic structure. It must seek to achieve both economic growth and broad, fair distribution of wealth. It is no simple task.

"WE HAVE LEARNED A LOT" [15]

Gardiner: When people are adjusting themselves to their new independence, they go through a process which can lead to upheavals—in fact, it has led to upheavals in many parts of Africa. The surprising thing is that the upheavals haven't been even more violent and more frequent.

When you allow for all this, one can say that in the past ten years, taking Congolese independence as the bench mark, we have learned a lot. The people with better training, the people who have grown more seasoned with experience, will begin to be more productive now at the beginning of the second United Nations Development Decade. Here we've got to draw distinctions. . . .

[15] From "Nation Building in Africa," an interview by Immanuel Wallerstein, professor of sociology at Columbia University, with Robert K. A. Gardiner, Ghanaian executive secretary of the United Nations Economic Commission for Africa. *War/Peace Report.* 9:3-5. Mr. '69. Reprinted by permission. Professor Wallerstein is the author of *Africa: Politics of Independence* and *Africa: Politics of Unity.*

In what I call the Middle Belt, from Mauritania to the Congo, the rate of economic growth has been lowest. Here the shortage of personnel has been very obvious, the fragmentation of the continent into smaller nations more pronounced, and therefore a high percentage of capital expenditure has been put into infrastructure—transport, power, telecommunications, and other devices—not only to create *international* economic links but even more to build the *national* market itself. For in most African countries if you are a few miles from the railway line, you're not in the exchange economy at all.

Q. What would you say has been the role of powers outside the African continent in the process of economic growth in the last ten years?

A. I don't think the former colonial powers have got used to the idea of their wards being independent; they have not isolated themselves or allowed themselves to be isolated. On the other hand, of course, some of the African countries have tended more or less to resign themselves to the patronage of their overlords. Then, too, some African nations have been excessively suspicious about anything coming from outside. Also, some have tried to find shortcuts through ideological dogma; some have believed that the economic process may take the form of a jump or a leap forward. . . .

Q. Would you speak to the specific functions of the Economic Commission for Africa in this process of development?

A. Naturally I see these developments through the eyes of ECA. We have provided a forum, a meeting place, a secretariat for the African governments, which have enabled them to examine their own problems, to explore methods of coping with these problems, and in some cases even to negotiate to tackle these problems. We have investigated, perhaps revealed, opportunities, in industry, power and agriculture, and this is something novel.

When Africans now take part in the work of global agencies like UNCTAD [United Nations Conference on Trade and Development] and UNIDO [United Nations Industrial

Development Organization], they are aware of two things:
that there is a world problem as well as an African problem
—and a solution of world problems may not mean a solution
of African problems; and secondly, that they are participating in international economic discussions as responsible
members of the international economic community, not as
camp-followers. For example, some people have considered
overseas aid a blessing in every form, but this is not the
attitude that has been encouraged by the ECA. We think in
terms of the inflow of foreign resources and the resultant
outflow in foreign exchange and where potentially—or even
actually—these countries can earn enough to pay for these
imports, we have got to examine their effects. We must consider the initial loan and the repayment price, whether the
ratio can justify the transaction, and so on. Even a gift, a
total gift, can pose problems: If a country that hasn't got
enough resources is given an atomic reactor, it can spend its
whole budget just to maintain the reactor.

All this we see from our experiences. We are now doing
business, not just looking for *charity.* . . .

We are not going to isolate ourselves from the rest of the
world. Cooperation is not only correct, it's the only sensible
way. Nobody is coming to Africa to develop the continent
for our benefit. We have got to develop it ourselves, but
what comes from outside may be decisive. It will be decisive,
however, only if it is supplementary or complementary to
the efforts of the indigenous people.

Q. Would you say the actual patterns of international
trade between Africa and the rest of the world have changed
in the last ten years?

A. Not noticeably, but changes *are* taking place.

Q. What further changes would you expect over the next
ten years?

A. One very necessary condition for economic progress—
and this is what we are now saying in the ECA—is mass
consumption in Africa and mass employment. These will be
the indicators of change.

Q. What about priorities? How much progress have you made in thinking through where you work on education, on health, on industry, on agriculture—and the phasing of them together so that you don't end up just creating other problems at the same time?

A. People have talked about critical areas, decisive areas, and for some time certain of them were emphasized at the risk of excluding essential prior steps.

Education is a case in point. You can have a whole country of literate people without any employment opportunities. Some people even go to the extent of programming the educational system so as to produce the skills required, but even then you've got to make sure that the economy will develop in the direction of those skills. Health and population is another example—you can improve health conditions, even increase the population, but again that will create food shortages if agriculture does not advance at the same time.

So we in the ECA are not trying to deal with isolated factors. We're dealing with whole economies....

Let me just say in general, we are making mistakes, but we are not repeating mistakes. This is a question linking all the interests involved, the selfish as well as the objective, all the methods adopted, all the misunderstandings. People caught in the same net are at least able to ask, "Are we repeating these mistakes?" And you notice that in the discussions taking place from time to time, people try to draw a distinction between what is happening in this area and what happened in that other area. Every experience, however painful and expensive, has also been a lesson.

V. AFRICA, THE UNITED STATES, AND THE FUTURE

EDITOR'S INTRODUCTION

West Africa is not an island. Its future, for good or ill, will be influenced by its relations with its African neighbors and with the rest of the world, including the great powers.

In 1960 East and West appeared prepared to do battle to gain spheres of influence in Africa. Ten years later "no great power has been able to impose its will in Africa as fully as it might wish," notes R. W. Apple, Jr. Even the interest in imposing any will at all appears to have declined. In Washington, according to Professor Rupert Emerson of Harvard, Africa has again become the least considered of the continents.

Americans, like their Government, lack interest in Africa, and they also lack knowledge and understanding, writes Philip W. Quigg, former managing editor of *Foreign Affairs*. But he believes the tide will change in the coming decade. In the final selection, author-lecturer Basil Davidson places his hopes for Africa's future on African genius: "The world's experience may help. But the structures that are needed will have to stand on their own soil."

NEW ERA IN INTER-AFRICAN RELATIONS [1]

The end of the Nigerian civil war in January 1970, has opened a new era of inter-African relations.

The considerable attention focused on the role of the big powers in postwar Nigerian construction has given way

[1] Article, "Diplomatic Drums: Inter-African Contacts Quicken in Wake of Nigerian Civil War." *Christian Science Monitor.* p 4. Je. 4, '70. Reprinted by permission from *The Christian Science Monitor.* © 1970 The Christian Science Publishing Society. All rights reserved.

to many questions concerning the postwar diplomatic role of various African states.

The economic weakness and military strength of Nigeria, Africa's most populous country with almost 60 million inhabitants, has posed both potential threats and opportunities for neighboring states.

These possibilities center on economic competition within Africa and the size of the huge Nigerian market.

Competition for technological and cultural influence, which arose between the former British and French colonies at independence, continues. French support for secessionist Biafra through diplomatic recognition and aid by the Ivory Coast and Gabon are evidence of this competition. Thus the French-speaking states have lost access to the postwar Nigerian market, at least for the short term. But they have been busy consolidating their interests in other areas.

Unity Reasserted

A series of meetings of French-speaking countries in March, including the ministers of finance of the members of the franc zone in Abidjan, the Ivory Coast capital, and cultural associations in Niamey, the capital of Niger, were efforts to reassert Francophonic unity in the face of a reunited Nigeria.

These diplomatic contacts have been reinforced by high-level meetings between heads of state of the members of the Council of the Entente (Ivory Coast, Niger, Upper Volta, and Togo) at the Togolese independence ceremonies in Lomé on April 27. An earlier visit to Abidjan by Congolese Foreign Minister Cyrille Adoula to see President Félix Houphouët-Boigny was followed by a recent two-day visit by Congolese President Joseph Mobutu.

Perhaps the most important diplomatic contact, however, came between Prime Minister Kofi Busia of Ghana and President Houphouët-Boigny. In a well-orchestrated ten-day state visit to the neighboring Ivory Coast, Prime Minister Busia repeatedly affirmed Ghana's desire to strengthen West African unity and to enter into efforts at regional cooperation. A treaty of friendship, the abolition of visas for nationals visiting the two countries, and the formation of an Ivorian-Ghanaian commission to encourage common development projects and increased trade were all seen as important steps to affirm their strength in relation to Nigeria.

Distrust Fades

Both Ghana, which expelled many Nigerians in its October [1969] removal of unemployed foreign Africans from its territory, and the Ivory Coast, which still does not have diplomatic relations with Nigeria, have reason to be pleased that they have overcome the mutual distrust which existed during the rule of Kwame Nkrumah. Their overtures are also important because they come between states of different colonial heritages.

Another important development has come between France, the Ivory Coast, and the Republic of Guinea. Isolated since its breakaway from France in 1958, Guinea has been supported by a series of benefactors, including the Soviet Union, Communist China, and the United States, all in turn. Its economic and cultural interests, however, still remain with France and neighboring Francophonic states such as Senegal, Mali, or the Ivory Coast. While this reconciliation—evidenced in soccer games between the Ivory Coast and Guinea, or tentative friendly statements by French Foreign Minister Maurice Schumann—appears slow, it is extremely important for the development of West Africa because of Guinea's geographic location and its ideological stance.

Ivory Coast Prevails

Strongly socialist, Guinean President Sékou Touré has lost out economically to his rival in the Ivory Coast—now probably the most prosperous West Africa state. But he has managed to stay in power far longer than most African heads of state. Although a rumored meeting between Presidents

Touré and Houphouët-Boigny on their common frontiers on May 5 failed to materialize, there is speculation of increased contact in the near future.

These contacts fit into a larger picture of growing African diplomatic activity at the end of the first decade of independence. Unlike the first decade, the second promises more realistic diplomacy as the African leaders seem to better understand the interests of their countries within Africa.

Little improvement in the level of economic development, a deterioration in the terms of exchange with industrialized states, and a traumatic failure in diplomacy to halt the Nigerian civil war all contribute to the common view that African states need one another.

The past few months have shown that African governments agree and are ready to act to achieve their own purposes and to increasingly support the common good of all.

THE GREAT POWERS AND AFRICA [2]

During the Eisenhower Administration Vice President Richard M. Nixon submitted to the President a report describing the coming struggle between East and West in Africa.

His was not an isolated view. Many people foresaw the development of Communist and capitalist spheres of influence in Africa, perhaps even the appearance of satellite states, and American policy was largely rooted in a fear of Soviet or Chinese domination.

Ten years later it is clear that no great power has been able to impose its will in Africa as fully as it might wish.

The former colonial powers—Britain, France, Belgium and Spain—have retained considerable economic influence in the territories that were once their possessions. But the Belgians in the Congo, the British in Tanzania, the French

[2] From "Major Powers, Soviet and China Included, Find Influence in Africa Limited," by R. W. Apple, Jr., New York *Times* correspondent. New York *Times*. p 4. N. 26, '69. © 1969 by The New York Times Company. Reprinted by permission.

in Mali, have had to accept political and economic developments that they did not like.

French Position Strong

France has probably built the strongest position, with
troops still stationed in several African countries. There are
several reasons: the small size and economic feebleness of
most of her former colonies, General Charles de Gaulle's
gift for personal relations with African leaders and the appeal of French culture for the African elite.

The British created a large corps of civil servants in
their colonies; the French educated fewer people but turned
out black Frenchmen who love Bordeaux and Baudelaire.

But even France has had problems. To varying degrees,
countries like Mali, Guinea and the Congo Republic (Brazzaville) have veered off in directions that the French find
uncomfortable, and there is relatively little they can do
about it.

In fact, one of the most surprising developments in post-
independent black Africa has been the new countries' determination to find their own way, accepting help where
they can get it but making manifest their unwillingness to
accept domination.

Political Sophistication

For a time the Soviet Union and China made what appeared to Western analysts to be a major effort to establish
Communist or pro-Communist regimes. Ghana inclined in
their direction, as did Mali and Guinea, but Kwame Nkrumah was overthrown in Ghana, Modibo Keita was overthrown in Mali and Sékou Touré of Guinea has proved to
be a supple pragmatist.

The Africans have demonstrated considerable political
sophistication.

We know more than you think we do [said a Cabinet minister
in Mali a few months ago]. We know that the Americans and the
Russians and all the rest aren't giving us money because they love

us. We know that there are strings. But knowing that makes it easier for us to shrug and keep to what seems to us our own best policy.

One reason for communism's failure to take hold is the character of traditional African society. The strength of tribal ties and teachings—including land-ownership patterns—presents a barrier to Marxist thought, as does the instinct of hundreds of thousands of Africans for trade. It is not easy, a Nigerian official once commented, to implant communism in a nation of petty merchants.

A second reason is the surprising persistence of Western political ideals and forms, a legacy from the colonial era. Although one would be hard-pressed to find a functioning democracy, by European standards, on the continent, most African political leaders still consider a democratic system as a proper goal.

Faced with those realities, the Chinese and the Russians appear to have changed the emphasis of their African policies.

They are no longer so interested in installing leaders who will do their bidding; their chief goal now seems to be to win the confidence of established governments. . . .

The United States has its allies in Africa, of course, such as Liberia and Ethiopia. There also remains a small number of countries whose leaders are rigorously anti-Communist (President H. Kamazu Banda of Malawi likes to say that he would take help from the devil if it would help Malawi, but he is always careful to make it clear that "the devil" excludes China and the Soviet Union) .

But American policy is no longer as activist as it was in the early years. The period of chaos in the Congo, when the United States involved itself deeply in trying to restore pro-Western order, appears to have persuaded policy makers to adopt a somewhat more passive stance. The cautious and tentative American efforts to alleviate the sufferings of the Nigerian civil war are an example of the new stance.

So black Africa moves along its multiple paths, with half a dozen kinds of "African socialism," and all of them almost never doctrinaire regardless of the path chosen.

UNITED STATES POLICY [3]

American policy toward Africa in the era of independence can either be lauded as representing a sane, well-balanced, and responsible course of action, or downgraded as timid, unimaginative, and ill-attuned to African needs and aspirations. Which side of this controversy one chooses to take depends less upon the facts of the case—although which facts are selected may obviously be of crucial significance—than upon the assumptions and expectations from which one sets off.

As the United States played only a slight direct role in promoting the independence of African colonies, so it has generally lagged behind the more dynamic of African leaders who at least on anticolonial and racial issues could usually carry all or the bulk of Africa with them. A case can be made, indeed, for the proposition that the only extended period during which American policy and African nationalist aspirations were reasonably well in balance was during the first year or so of the Kennedy Administration when the African states were still tentatively feeling their way and the United States had taken a leap into more venturesome policies; but radical African nationalism soon left the United States behind again. Although John F. Kennedy's coming to office lent a freshness and new vitality to the American approach to Africa, the special glow imparted to the relationship by President Kennedy left little trace. It was not that Lyndon Johnson had any hostility to Africa, but only that the warm and intimate concern of his predecessor was gone. The appealing special interest which Washington had shown in Africa receded as Africa became again the least

[3] From *Africa and United States Policy*, by Rupert Emerson, professor of government, Harvard University. Prentice-Hall. '67. p 95-100. © 1967. By permission of Prentice-Hall, Inc., Englewood Cliffs, New Jersey.

considered of the continents; and Africa was soon aware of the change. . . .

As more and more African states came on the scene and their policies became more sharply differentiated, it was increasingly obvious that no single line of American policy could hope to satisfy everybody. "Our purpose and policy is plain," asserted Assistant Secretary of State [G. Mennen] Williams in 1961. "We want for Africa what the Africans want for themselves," a proposition which was feasible when the Africans appeared to be of one mind but which became problematical when they disagreed among themselves. The cleavage, for example, between the more left-oriented, "progressive" states of the Guinea-Ghana-Mali stripe and the more conservative position of many of the rest forced the United States to pick and choose, thus inevitably disaffecting some and usually precisely those who spoke up most vociferously. . . .

Nor was this only a question as between states, since the same issues in varying degrees divided the citizenry within many of the African countries. Thus in Nigeria a sizable proportion of the politically minded in the Southern regions repudiated the conservatism of the Northern-dominated government in Lagos, an attitude which played at least a subsidiary role in the military coup of January 1966, engineered in the first instance primarily by Ibo officers. Ghana's corresponding coup in the succeeding month represented a takeover by moderate or conservative forces which repudiated Nkrumah's radicalism.

It also became more and more evident that some of the policies which Africans advocated with growing intransigence by no means necessarily laid out courses of action which the United States was prepared to pursue. Where African leaders passionately sought drastic and immediate action, the United States was inclined to counsel caution and slow motion. . . .

African-American relations have been rendered more difficult and given the appearance of being more intractable than they actually are by the tendency on both sides to clothe in high moral terms the positions taken on major issues. Africa's spokesmen are inclined to attribute moral validity only to their own strongly-held views on colonial and racial matters or the need for development, and to blame anything which goes wrong on the imperialists. The corresponding American touchstone is the degree and depth of anti-Communist commitment, with the implication that those who give other questions higher priority, as virtually all Africans do, are either blind or dupes of the archenemy.

These are, of course, in some measure caricatures of American and African positions, but they possess enough of reality to point up homely truths. As the United States has been inclined to look under the bed for Communists, so Africans have clung to the illusion of a natural harmony of African interests, if the imperialists will only leave them alone. Thus Nkrumah wanted all tribalism cast out of Ghana's national life: "We are all Africans and peoples of African descent, and we shall not allow the imperialist plotters and intriguers to separate us from each other for their own advantage." In the same vein, Julius Nyerere, pleading for pan-Africanism, asserted that "We must use African national states as an instrument for the unification of Africa, and not allow our enemies to use them as tools for dividing Africa." What is missing is recognition that African peoples and states, like those everywhere in the world, are quite capable of falling out among themselves without the need of some alien evil genius to destroy their harmony, and that outsiders may disagree with Africans without necessarily being enemies.

This is not intended to deny that anyone who is so inclined, as are numbers of Asians and Africans, can produce documented evidence to support the charge that the imperialists remain unreconciled to the successes of the colonial liberation movement. Even leaving aside the more subtle manipulations of neocolonialism, the anti-imperialists can point to a long series of overt events, such as the Anglo-

French attack on Egypt in the Suez crisis, the French colonial wars in Indochina and Algeria, the violent clash between France and Tunisia in 1961 over the naval base at Bizerte, and the armed intervention of France in Gabon in 1964 to rescue President Léon M'ba from overthrow, the escalating American war in Vietnam and the affairs of Cuba and the Dominican Republic. . . . These are all matters which are clear on the record. How much weight should they be given, particularly when balanced against the equally plain fact that hundreds of millions of colonial peoples have won or been conceded their freedom? Imperialism of the old style is far nearer to being dead than its critics and its enemies often give it credit for being.

As a general rule, it is more realistic to assume that disagreements between African countries or between them and the United States are not ordinarily caused by sinister alien forces but rather reflect significant differences in the position of states and in their estimate as to how best to safeguard and promote their interests. It is folly to think that in a continent as vast and diverse as Africa all peoples would see eye to eye or that serious divergences would not from time to time divide African states from a country as remote and differently situated as the United States. Even with full American sympathy and good will for Africa, there is no reason to assume that the American national interest will necessarily coincide with the African interest, although the potential range of coincidence seems great.

Disinterest or Indifference?

The United States can still in large part follow a disinterested policy in relation to Africa in the sense that its specific interests continue to be relatively slight and that it is still not closely identified with particular African countries. Since the American economic interest is of no outstanding significance, amounting for the entire continent to less than 5 per cent of the total American foreign trade and investment, any interpretation of American policy which derives primarily from economic factors has a ring of improbability to it; nor is there reason to believe that the drive of American economic interests to establish themselves in Africa is so great and persuasive as to exercise a dominant influence on American policy.

It is consistent with both the basic American policy of anticommunism and other American purposes more congenial to the Africans that the United States should follow policies which may legitimately be characterized as benevolent. By fortunate accident it happens that the American national interest, as a general proposition, is served by African economic, social, and political development, by moves designed to promote African collaboration and unity, and by the maintenance of peace in the continent—all, of course, to be carried forward under non-Communist auspices. To anyone partial to the left-wing charges that the United States is the archimperialist, seeking only to dominate Africa in order to exploit it more fully, such a statement as this must seem either ridiculously naïve or wantonly corrupt; and yet it is arguable that the primary American sin in Africa is not that it has so grossly intervened in African affairs but that it has so often regarded Africa as one of its peripheral concerns to which it need pay little consecutive attention. If American intentions are good, and even reasonably honorable, it is also true that they bear low priority and have little steam behind them. African development is seen as desirable on all counts, but it is not a matter to which major American resources are currently to be devoted.

As Arnold Rivkin has put it, "our unwillingness to take more initiative in Africa is the more remarkable because it is the one area in the world in which the United States has more freedom of action and fewer constraints on its foreign-policy making than in any other." Regrettably, a disinterested policy can be an indifferent one as well.

Furthermore, the disinterested character of American policy toward Africa ensures neither that that policy will be wise nor that it will fit in with what the Africans see as their interests. It is evident that the United States has many interests which do not directly concern Africa, and inevitably some of them will run counter to African desires. For the most part, to be sure, Washington can follow policies in relation to Africa which are explicitly framed to deal with African problems and needs, but from time to time conflicts of interest prove unavoidable. Operationally, in Washington terms, the issue has often posed itself in contrary courses of action advocated by the African, as opposed to the European, desks in the State Department, forcing decision at a higher level where the concerns of Africa are only one element, and sometimes only a negligible element, in the total picture. Certainly it is true that there is no reason why the European desks should take priority on matters primarily concerning Africa, but it is equally true that the African interest must occasionally give way.

A case can be made for the proposition that in many, perhaps in most, spheres there is no occasion for any sharp divergence of interest between the United States and African countries, but African-American relations are bound to be rendered difficult and touchy by the basic contrast between American wealth, power, advancement, and attachment to private enterprise on one side and African poverty, weakness, backwardness, and attachment to socialism on the other. . . .

In sum, Africa has risen greatly in the American scheme of things in the last decade, but it must still inevitably compete with other parts of the world which the United States views with greater and more continuous concern.

THE CHANGING AMERICAN VIEW OF AFRICA [4]

Before there can be understanding, there must be interest. Are Americans interested in Africa?

It is now trite to say that until about fifteen years ago the average American's view of Africa had been shaped almost

[4] Article by Philip W. Quigg, formerly managing editor of *Foreign Affairs*. *Africa Report*. 14:8-11. Ja. '69. Reprinted by permission of Africa Report Magazine.

entirely by Tarzan movies. Africans have every reason to resent the crazily distorted image that was created, but it was not without positive elements. Along with the illusion that the most interesting thing in Africa was its animal life, that Africans were primitive, and that everything south of the Sahara was tropical rain forest, there were some more central simplifications: Europeans in Africa were invariably evil and out to exploit the Africans in the most devious and criminal ways; Africans were innocent and good; and Americans, who were also innocent and good (Americans totally identified with Tarzan, who was played by a succession of famous American athletes), would save the Africans from the ruthless Europeans. It is sometimes overlooked that these impressions made it easier for Americans to understand the African's resentment of Europeans and his sense of having been exploited; and, for good or ill, it made it easier for Americans to intervene in the affairs of Africa—including the application of pressure on the colonial powers to grant independence. (Let those who are still unconvinced remember that it was the white Tarzan who beat his chest and swung through the trees like a monkey—not the Africans.)

By the mid-1950s, some rays of light began to penetrate our almost total ignorance of the real situation in Africa, and interest became intense during the next decade. Our imaginations were caught up in the excitement of millions of people achieving self-determination and independence in the space of a few short years. The independence movements appealed to our conservative revolutionary tradition that there should be self-government achieved, by and large, in an orderly way. Anyone who knew anything at all about Africa was in wide demand as speaker and prophet of what was to happen next in a continent fairly exploding with activity. Young social scientists were rushing into the field of African studies and in the early 1960s our universities were training four or five times as many Africanists as Latin Americanists—an area of much older and more direct concern.

What Americans learned in that decade, and the body of expert knowledge which was rapidly built up by a few, should not be minimized. If we as a people are still appallingly ignorant of Africa, it is hardly surprising. We started from zero; whether we are notably more ignorant of Africa than of Asia or Latin America is moot. In the last analysis all people, as a whole, know little that is beyond their immediate ken—even within their own countries. What distinguishes Americans is that, because of their power and the responsibilities they have (rightly or wrongly) assumed after years of isolation, they have a particular obligation to be well informed and to comprehend the aspirations that are creating new and potent forces in the world.

Our performance has been spotty—and not merely with regard to Africa. The ignorance of our legislators is often beyond belief—until one examines the variety of subjects on which a congressman needs to be well informed and remembers the time consumed in serving the immediate interests of constituents as a means of staying in office. We have been slow to realize that education in the Hebraic-Greek-Christian tradition is not enough, that there are other cultures deserving our attention and understanding. The delay in translating that realization into substantial changes in school curricula is caused at least partly by the fact that knowledge in all areas is increasing geometrically. Even if inertia can be overcome, it is not easy to decide what should be added to, what taken from, school curricula.

But change is coming; it has been in progress for nearly three decades in our colleges and universities in response to natural intellectual curiosity and a less parochial world outlook following decades of isolation. There is now increasing attention to Africa in our schools, largely in response to the demands of our Afro-Americans and a growing awareness among white Americans that we cannot ignore the history and traditions of 10 per cent of our population.

Sources of Information About Africa

What part has the press played in informing Americans about Africa? Many Africans are indignant with the foreign press coverage of their countries and believe that it is largely responsible for the misunderstanding of Africa in the United States and elsewhere. No doubt there has been some irresponsible, even malicious, reporting. Sensationalism and an emphasis on failures rather than achievements have characterized much of the writing from Africa. But this is a world-wide complaint and has been the subject of endless controversy within as well as between countries for as long as there has been a fourth estate. Americans, too, can become very sensitive to the fact that in the press of most countries the United States is rarely mentioned except in a context of (1) racism, (2) materialism, or (3) imperialism.

By almost any standard, foreign reporting is everywhere inadequate in quantity as well as quality. This is almost inevitable. There are too many countries and there is too little public interest. Such interest as there is will invariably focus more on, say, an ugly civil war in Nigeria than on a progressive social revolution in Tanzania. It is true, too, that most foreign correspondents are not adequately trained for their assignments and, if they are roving away from their base, generally spend too little time in the countries through which they are junketing.

Nevertheless, my own opinion is that reporting from Africa for American newspapers has been, on balance, above average and has done much more to help than to hurt African interests. The reason is quite simply that beneath the displays of cynicism or churlishness, which are widely cherished affectations of journalists, the vast majority of American newspapers and correspondents have been fundamentally sympathetic to black Africa. As a result, the main lines of the Africa story have, I think, got through to the American people, even if superficially. And the best of the reporting from Africa has been superlative, not only in newspapers, but also on television. More disturbing than the distortions or sensation-seeking of some correspondents is the fact that, as the high drama of newly won independence recedes, substantive (as contrasted to crisis) reporting from Africa appears to be declining.

No less important than the press in forming impressions of Africa have been Africans themselves—students studying in America, representatives at the United Nations, and African leaders visiting the United States in an official or unofficial capacity. Their effectiveness as ambassadors of Africa has been in almost direct proportion to their candor in defining the real problems of their countries and what it is specifically they are trying to accomplish. Where, as so often, they have shown dignity, high intelligence, and a capacity to articulate the aspirations of Africans, they have made an enormous impression on Americans and done more than anything else could to create understanding. No doubt Africans from the non-English-speaking countries are at some disadvantage in this regard (though [Guinean President] Sékou Touré caught the imagination of the American people as few visitors have), yet in considerable measure the Africans who are most fluent in English can and do speak for all.

I particularly remember a visit of Tom Mboya [the late economics minister of Kenya, slain in 1969] when he was only twenty-nine and little known in the United States. His brilliance in debate with the crusty journalists of the television program "Meet the Press" and on a dozen other occasions changed many opinions about Africans. How many of our own at that age, Americans asked, could handle themselves with so much poise and intelligence? Similarly, the quiet sincerity of a Julius Nyerere [Tanzanian president] and the restrained strength of a Kenneth Kaunda [Zambian president], on visits to the United States, have helped to create a respect for African leadership essential to sympathetic understanding. I have always regretted that Jomo Kenyatta has never visited us because I believe he would captivate Americans and be a supremely effective spokesman of Africa. The patient work of men such as Ghana's Alex Quaison-Sackey and Nigeria's Chief Simeon Adebo at the United Nations have also made Americans more aware of Africa as a force in the world. (At the risk of appearing to take a self-interested view, I should like to add my opinion that African leaders underestimate the value of writing for serious American journals as a means of creating understanding in America. I know what heavy pressures they are under, but a carefully thought-out and candid article, which will receive wide attention in the press and be widely reprinted, is the next best thing to an official visit and consumes far less time and energy.)

Groups With Special Interest in Africa

Yet the fact remains that Africa is poorly understood by most Americans and seems to them remote from America's fundamental national interests. At present, Africa has perhaps five identifiable constituencies in the United States—that is, five groups which, for good or for ill, take a special interest in Africa.

The first is composed of academic and professional people, with a scattering of businessmen. They are well informed about Africa, whether or not they are professionally involved with it; they are concerned, inclined to be liberal, and have considerable influence in the executive branch of the Government. About 90 per cent of the Americans who are really knowledgeable about Africa are found in this group. Their numbers are small—perhaps 10,000—but their understanding of Africa represents the basis of such wisdom as we have been able to muster in our attitudes and policies toward Africa.

The second constituency is composed of the Afro-American. Until recently, his interest in, and identification with, Africa have been limited and isolated. The work of the American Colonization Society which led to the creation of Liberia, of Marcus Garvey and W. E. B. Du Bois, of the handful of Negro intellectuals involved in the development of the pan-African movement—these are historically important but had little impact on the mass of American Negroes. Now, of course, attitudes are changing. In their new self-awareness, many Afro-Americans (even the term *Negro* is now resented as having colonial-era overtones) are taking pride in their color and in their culture, of which they have been largely unaware or actively deprived. Even today, however, the majority of black Americans searching for identity and self-respect look more to their antecedents in America than in Africa. Moreover, those who must struggle hardest for existence, who are most preoccupied with getting from today to tomorrow, are least likely to be concerned with things outside their immediate sphere. To be well informed about Africa is still a luxury reserved primarily for the well-educated. Therefore knowledge of Africa among Negroes is still rudimentary and their interest uneven. They are not yet a substantial influence in the making of American policy toward Africa—though no one doubts that the time is approaching when the 20 million Americans of African descent will carry great political weight on issues involving Africa.

The third identifiable group with some sense of involvement with Africa is typified by the church-going Middlewesterner, whose interests are humanitarian rather than political, social, or economic. Like his father before him, he supports Christian missions in Africa without knowing much about the continent. His view of Africa tends to be romantic, sentimental, and dated, but his instincts are right and he represents the backbone of that sometime majority of Americans who supported aid to less developed countries. If his children are young and in school, they probably know considerably more facts about Africa than he does, and also share their parents' sense of responsibility and concern for those less fortunate than themselves.

The fourth group is characterized by the average American businessman with interests or markets in Africa. He professes to be apolitical, is chary of giving his opinion, and favors whatever status quo prevails, whether it be of the left or right. Because he is likely to have worldwide involvements, he may have no particular interest in Africa beyond the preservation of a climate in which he can achieve an adequate return on his investment. He is a conservative force, but not a reactionary one.

The fifth group consists of rightists and racist organizations whose primary concerns may be domestic, but who profess to find in Africa an object lesson in the virtues of segregation and white supremacy. With South Africa and Rhodesia they have a lovefeast; and each takes in the other's dirty linen. The millions of dollars that South Africa spends in the United States to brainwash Americans would be ineffectual without these right-wing groups; conversely, the South Africans represent them at home as the authentic voice of the American people. In fact, their numbers are small, but their resources are great.

Of course, these groups are far more complex and variegated than I have suggested. Even so, they constitute a pretty fragile base on which to build a real understanding of Africa among the American people. Perhaps the most that can be said is that the purposes of four of the five groups are constructive and consistent with the interests of Africa.

Reasons for Decline of Interest

What should be of more concern than the lack of understanding of Africa among Americans is the decline of interest, on which the acquisition of understanding so much depends. The reasons for this decline are many:

First, it was probably inevitable that the acute interest of the early 1960s could not be sustained; the drama of these years was inherently exceptional. Second, Americans have become disillusioned with foreign aid and its promise of promoting rapid economic development. The academic experts and Government administrators who oversold foreign aid share much of the blame for this disillusionment, but judgments should not be too harsh. The initial overenthusiasm of the developmental economists is understandable, and so is the waning of public enthusiasm when the miracles failed to occur. Successive administrations in Washington were induced to make ever more extravagant claims for foreign aid to persuade a reluctant Congress to appropriate adequate funds, and so the cycle continued. As Africans know better than most, development is a long, slow process.

Third, Americans have increasingly felt that they were carrying disproportionately heavy burdens. The average American is not impressed by the knowledge that his is the wealthiest country in the world. When Federal, state, and local governments take a quarter or a half (or even more) of his income in taxes, he feels very poor in terms of *his* rising expectations, and increasingly let down by allied nations which seem to be carrying less and less of the costs of mutual defense. Since the European powers have a prior and more immediate interest in Africa, why not let them carry the major burden of that continent's aid requirements? The fact remains that the decline in foreign-aid appropriations is a national disgrace; it can be explained but not excused.

A fourth reason for declining interest in Africa arises from a growing uncertainty as to how we can effectively help. We have grown much more skeptical in the last few years about our capacity to give useful advice, and more dubious about our power to affect the destiny of Africa. To most Americans who think about such problems at all, Southern Africa seems beyond solution, even if we had the political will —which we clearly don't. In the Congo, we earned the gratitude of no one at great cost to ourselves. The selfish interests which others saw in our policies and actions there are totally obscure to most Americans. Weren't we the only power which consistently supported the integrity of the Congo as a nation, regardless of the personalities who at one time or another were allied with us for their own purposes? Yet we were vilified at various times by Europeans and Africans alike for supporting or opposing particular political figures deemed admirable or unsavory by those with political or financial interests of their own. The experience is not one that Americans want to repeat soon again.

Fifth, Americans have been disappointed by the performance of the new African nations—their instability, the infringement of democratic rights, the corruption of many leaders of promise. No doubt attention has focused more on Africa's shortcomings than on its achievements, and no doubt, too, expectations were impossibly high. Why Americans should have expected more of Africans than of others with more experience is difficult to explain. To the extent there was any rationality in this attitude, it probably rested on the hope that, because Africa did not have the ancient oligarchies and class consciousness of, say, Latin America, it might escape those political pressures and tensions which inhibit progress for all the people. However unwarranted the expectations held or the judgments passed, it must be recognized that Nkrumah and his kind hurt Africa badly.

Our preoccupation with Vietnam hardly needs to be labored as a sixth reason for the declining interest in Africa. It has consumed our energies and attention. But what is more important, it has opened up a serious debate as to what our proper role in the world may be. If the lesson of Vietnam is misread by Americans, the United States may turn into itself in ways that will have a profound effect on Africa as well as other continents. At the very least, it is likely to be a long time before we engage our forces abroad—certainly outside the Western Hemisphere. But perhaps the deepest impact of Vietnam is to have focused attention as never before on our domestic problems, and this is the final and most important reason for a declining interest in Africa.

For the first time since World War II, we are more concerned with poverty and unrest at home than abroad. We are more involved with achieving freedom and justice for all of our own people than for Africans in Rhodesia or South Africa—or anyone else. We have a whole litany of inter-related domestic problems—air and water pollution, urban sprawl, crime, slums—which we seem disposed for the first time to tackle seriously. Congress will continue to back and fill in appropriating adequate funds and we will make many mistakes, as we have abroad. But action there will be, and it will consume a great part of our energy and attention. In consequence, there will be less for Africa—less money, less interest, less concern, and probably less understanding. At least it will look that way to Africans.

Does Familiarity Bring Understanding?

I have been dwelling more on knowledge and interest than understanding, for the first two are prerequisites for the third, though they do not necessarily assure it. Furthermore, "understanding" is not easy to define, much less achieve. Is it a purely intellectual process or does it require empathy and a sense of mutual involvement? Certainly familiarity is not enough. For example, the white American is just beginning to understand the Afro-American, with whom he has been in contact for a couple of hundred years (though to be sure it has been far less time in the northern and western parts of the country).

On the other hand, one of the great myths cherished by the majority of Americans, and shared by many others, is that, if understanding between peoples can be achieved, problems between them will vanish, mutual respect will flower, and tranquillity will reign throughout the world. This, of course, is sentimental nonsense. Understanding *may* sharpen differences and accentuate problems. Surveys have consistently shown that African students studying in the United States departed with a lower opinion of us than when they arrived. It might be argued that they left with greater familiarity but still without understanding. If so—and it would be a rash American who made the contention—it only demonstrates how difficult understanding is to achieve.

In this somewhat pessimistic analysis of American interest and understanding of Africa, I have neglected one important and positive element. There are fewer barriers to American understanding of Africa than of Asia or Latin America. Africans and Americans share a certain absence of sophistication found in older cultures, a directness in manner, an unfocused energy, an easy good humor. How much our attitudes and values have been shaped toward those of Africa by that substantial minority among us which came from Africa is hard to say, so diverse are our ethnic origins and cross-fertilization of cultures. But clearly it is not enough to point out our common musical roots and let it go at that. Our conscious and unconscious attempt to isolate the Negro has obscured the impact he has had on our culture and even, I suspect, our collective personality. What is clear beyond doubt is that the black American is central to the issue of understanding between Africa and the United States. We cannot expect sympathetic understanding of Africans except as we knuckle down to our racial problem; we will not have sufficient sympathetic understanding of Africa until we have solved it. Meanwhile, the Afro-American is nonetheless a positive link between us.

The very beginning of understanding is the will and the capacity to put oneself in the other fellow's place and thus, as it were, to get inside him. This is rare enough as between individuals, much less nations. In these terms it is doubtful that any people understands any other people; only certain individuals have the desire and the ability and these become the invaluable interpreters of other nations to their own countrymen. By this measure, Africa is well served in America. The question is: How many people are listening?

Today, all too few. But it may not and need not always be so. At the moment we are unquestionably preoccupied as never before with our own external and internal problems. We are in a selfish and inward-looking mood; even the idealism of our young people, which a decade ago was markedly outward looking, is today focused in other directions and is wary of any kind of foreign involvement, even the most beneficent. But I would guess that within the coming decade the tide will change again. The new impulse will be humanitarian; it will also be intensely practical, and hopefully freed from cold-war considerations. When we have put our own house in better order, when we have redefined our worldwide responsibilities and seen them in better proportion, I believe we will come more fully to recognize that our nation cannot prosper indefinitely amidst poverty, that what we will by then have begun to attain for all our citizens—enough to eat, equal justice, a sense of individual dignity—are so basic that they must be sought for everyone, however difficult the task. Then we will renew our interest in Africa—and perhaps enhance our understanding.

AFRICA'S FUTURE [5]

What kind of Africa may now emerge, what modern variant of an old civilization? . . .

The upheavals of the late 1960s were not the fruit of accident, bad luck or human incapacity, but of a crisis long in the making, a crisis of institutions on a continental scale. Its early signs may be found in some regions soon after 1800; in others, perhaps, as far back as the massive export of captives after 1650. Masked or delayed in precolonial times by the repeated adaptation of traditional institutions, this is also a crisis that was often deepened by the dismantlement of the colonial period.

It is furthermore a crisis whose ideological confusion has been again enlarged by various illusions. Many people outside Africa, and some within, have mistakenly believed that the colonial period not only swept away the old but also, like the English industrial revolution, laid foundations for the new. Any balanced survey of the evidence will now reveal that it achieved the first but not the second. All that emerged from the colonial period, in a structural sense, was an institutional void concealed for a while behind a political safety-curtain painted with parliamentary symbols of European provenance, a mere facade of order on lines drawn by alien cultures.

[5] From *The African Genius: An Introduction to African Cultural and Social History*, by Basil Davidson, lecturer and author of numerous books on African history and culture. (Atlantic Monthly Press Book) Little, Brown and Co. '70. p 313-17. Copyright © 1969 by Basil Davidson, published in England under title: *The Africans*. Reprinted by permission of Atlantic-Little, Brown and Co.

To most of those behind this curtain it might be distressingly clear that the old structures were in collapse, and that no new ones of enduring value had arrived to take their place. Most of those in front of the curtain were content to think otherwise. They learned better after the curtain had gone up, on the day of independence, and the elites of Western European and American training were duly embarked on their allotted roles. Soon a growing tumult could be heard in the wings. Soon this tumult rushed on stage.

This is not, I know, how a majority of colonial observers have understood the drama. For them the colonial period was constructive because it was thought to have conducted Africans into the modern world, and deliberately laid down the road to African equality with the rest of mankind. I do not myself belong to this "cheerful school" of colonial historians. The parallel, it seems to me, is once again with Britain. There too we have had a "cheerful school" of thought about the industrial revolution. The laboring poor may have continually rebelled against the poverty and squalor of industrialism: in truth, we are told, their sufferings were less than the blessings they received. Their average standard of living, on this view, went on rising all through the industrial revolution. And so it should follow, *sous entendu*, that the case for capitalism has been comfortably made.

Others have questioned these reassuring wage statistics. They have seen greater meaning in all those desperate acts of self-defense— the machine smashing and the workers' combinations, a myriad riots and upheavals. They have believed that the consequences of the industrial revolution were typical of "the first impact of new economic patterns, [which] threaten or disrupt the previous social relationships, while not immediately supplying new security devices in their place"; and that the industrial revolution really did produce "a catastrophic dislocation of the lives of the common people."

We have had the same division of opinion about what happened in Africa. Here too the cheerful school has greatly flourished. Their belief that civilization—whether as law, order, morality, or even history itself—essentially began with European rule may be found in great raftloads of books written in the last fifty years, and still being written. These views may now be seen to have ignored the evidence of history, and their interpretations to have been factitious. All those wars of self-defense, bitter rebellions, antiwitchcraft movements, millennial uprisings and a million individual acts of protest were set airily aside as the mere product of benighted savagery, perverted superstition or natural foolishness. All those new urban slums, miseries, moral squalors were explained, when they were explained at all, as the outcome of African fecklessness, incompetence or worse. And so with the post-independence upheavals: excellent institutions, it was said, had been provided—whose fault but African incapacity if they now failed to work?

In face of this kind of handling of the evidence one might perhaps argue polemically if impolitely the force of . . . [an] Asante proverb: . . . When many mice dig a hole, it does not become deep. The fact remains that the hole dug by the cheerful school has proved a pretty wide pit for educated Africans. No few of them have tumbled into it, and come to think that colonialism was institutionally a positive as well as a negative force, and that it really marked the beginning of civilization in Africa.

Not all such Africans have fallen into the pit: here too the cheerful school has had its critics. "From whichever angle you look at the first year of independence," commented a Nigeria headmaster in 1960, "you are faced with the stark reality of the fact that we were never, ideologically, prepared for independence." In many cases, remarked a qualified engineer somewhat later, "methods of winning independence and plans for the future have had no kind of theoretical basis, and, what is more, have been more or less detached from actual realities." And the weight of evidence seems mightily to support them.

From another standpoint, this is also a crisis of growth. In several senses: most strikingly, perhaps, in that of population. For reasons not yet explained but which can be only in some part due to preventive medicine, the rate of natural increase has gone steeply upward for several decades. Few reliable statistics are to hand, yet they all point this way. Sample statistics put the rate of natural increase in the Belgian Congo, for example, at as low as 0.6 per cent a year in 1932, and 1 per cent in 1945: by 1957, however, it had reached 2.3 per cent. Careful reviews have argued that by the middle 1960s the rate had risen to about 2.4 per cent a year for the whole continent. At the same time other evidence suggests that the rate of expansion in food supply cannot now maintain the average standard of living even at its present low general level.

With the pressing likelihood of total population again redoubled by the year 2000 or so, Africa for the first time confronts the prospect of chronic famine. The rich countries' aid seems unlikely to do anything serious about this: as commentators were noting in 1968, the rich countries appear no longer capable of rescuing the Third World reformism they have sponsored and at least verbally cherished. Perhaps, in a certain harsh way, it may prove to be as well. Most authorities agree that nothing can avert disaster in Africa except an accelerating rise in African productivity. But no such rise is possible without a great change in rural attitudes; and any such change must call in turn for radical shifts in socioeconomic structure, both within Africa and within the relationship between African economies and the rest of the world.

Other fields also display the growth aspects of this crisis. In all of them the answer seems to be the same: nothing but major structural change can now complete the work of transition.

By the late 1960s, for example, the concept of the sovereign and separate nation-state inherited from Europe was already in trouble. The building and maintaining of some forty such states had begun to wreck itself on two great reefs: first, that it could take far too little account of the ethnic particularities of many of these states; secondly, that many of them were in any case too small or too poor to be viable as sovereign and separate entities. The one great attempt at federation—in Nigeria—had gone far towards ruin through the rivalry of its constituent elites. Manifestly federation still held the key: just as clearly it would have to be federation on a structural basis far more popular than elitist rule could apparently provide.

Again one may cite the small but so instructive case of Guinea-Bissau [Portuguese Guinea]. To build an independent state out of five or more ethnic groups in the same colony can obviously make good sense. Yet these total fewer than a million people. Can it make good sense to try to build them into a *nation*-state? Obviously not, according to the experience of others, by proceeding on the elitist assumptions of European example. But, if not, then how marry their group independence, vital to any progress, to a due regard on one hand for the needs of their separate cultures and, on the other, for the needs of a wider unity with neighbors? Such questions began to be asked with a new urgency as the problems of reorganization became increasingly acute. Generalizing in some words of Julius Nyerere's in 1968, how build "a union of African states—a transfer of some sovereignty from our national units to a single unit of which we are all part ... [and so, among other things] coordinate and facilitate the economic development of Africa as a whole, in such a manner as to ensure the well-being of every part of the continent," conserving the many-colored fabric of African civilization while greatly strengthening and enlarging it? Or how transform, at other levels, the old methods of representation into new methods capable of integrating the rural millions into everyday political life? How devise structures of economic participation such as can enthuse and energize these rural millions, and so call forth work and sacrifice intense enough to change the future? How protect the chances of African economic expansion from world "terms of trade"—essentially, the falling value of African exports in terms of African imports—which have worked, and still work, so harshly against the interests of the Third World?

In the end it will be a matter of knowing how the civilization of the past can be remade by a new and bold vision. The Africans sorely need their modern revolution: profound and far-reaching in creative stimulus, unleashing fresh energies, opening new freedoms. The world's experience may help. But the structures that are needed will have to stand on their own soil. Perhaps this is only another way of saying that these new structures, as and when they emerge, will be nourished by the vigor and resilience of native genius, by all the inheritance of self-respect and innovating confidence that has carried these peoples through past centuries of change and cultural expansion.

BIBLIOGRAPHY

An asterisk (*) preceding a reference indicates that the article or a part of it has been reprinted in this book.

BOOKS, PAMPHLETS, AND DOCUMENTS

Abshire, D. M. and Samuels, M. A. eds. Portuguese Africa: a handbook. Praeger. '69.

Addona, A. F. The Organization of African Unity. World Publishing. '69.

Andreski, Stanislav. The African predicament: a study in the pathology of modernisation. Atherton. '68.

Awolowo, Obafemi. The strategy and tactics of the People's Republic of Nigeria. Macmillan. '70.

Aynor, H. S. Notes from Africa. Praeger. '69.

Barnes, Leonard. African renaissance. Bobbs. '69.

Bayliss, J. F. ed. Black slave narratives. Macmillan. '70.

Beier, Ulli. Contemporary art in Africa. Praeger. '68.

Bienen, Henry. The military intervenes: case studies in political development. Russell Sage. '68.

*Booth, Richard. The armed forces of African states, 1970. (Adelphi Papers no 67) Institute for Strategic Studies. 18 Adam St. London WC2N 6AL. '70.
  Reprinted in this volume: Introduction. William Gutteridge. p 4-5.

Butwell, Richard, ed. Foreign policy and the developing nation. University of Kentucky Press. '69.

Carter, G. M. and Paden, Ann, eds. Expanding horizons in African studies. Northwestern University Press. '69.

Cartey, Wilfred and Kilson, Martin, eds. The Africa reader: independent Africa. Random House. '70.

Church, R. J. H. Environment and policies in West Africa. Van Nostrand. '67.

*Cowan, L. G. The dilemmas of African independence. rev. ed. Walker. '68.

Crowder, Michael and Ikime, Obaro, eds. West African chiefs: their changing status under colonial rule and independence. Africana. '70.

Daggs, Elisa. All Africa; all its political entities of independent or other status. Hastings House. '70.

Daily Times (Nigeria). Nigeria yearbook, 1970. Daily Times. Lagos. '70.

*Davidson, Basil. The African genius: an introduction to African cultural and social history. (Atlantic Monthly Press Book) Little, Brown. '70.
  Published in England in 1969 under title: The Africans.

Davidson, Basil. The liberation of Guiné; aspects of an African revolution. Penguin. '69.

Davies, Oliver. West Africa before the Europeans. Methuen. '67.

Doro, M. E. and Stultz, N. M. eds. Governing in black Africa; perspectives on new states. Prentice-Hall. '70.

Dostert, P. E. Africa 1970. Stryker-Post Publications. 888 17th St. N.W. Washington, D.C. 20006. '70.

*Du Bois, V. D. Military rule and its repercussions in West Africa. (West Africa Series. v 12, no 6) American Universities Field Staff, Inc. Box 150. Hanover, N.H. 03755. '69.

Du Bois, V. D. The struggle for stability in the Upper Volta: pt. 4, Foreign reaction to the overthrow of President Maurice Yaméogo. (West Africa Series. v 12, no 4) American Universities Field Staff, Inc. Box 150. Hanover, N.H. 03755. '69.

Du Bois, V. D. The struggle for stability in the Upper Volta: pt. 5, The military regime of President Sangoulé Lamizana. (West Africa Series. v 12, no 5) American Universities Field Staff, Inc. Box 150. Hanover, N.H. 03755. '69.

Dumont, René. False start in Africa; tr. by P. N. Ott. 2d ed. rev. Praeger. '69.

Eicher, C. K. Research on agricultural development in five English-speaking countries in West Africa. Agricultural Development Council. 630 Fifth Ave. New York 10020. '70.

*Emerson, Rupert. Africa and United States policy. Prentice-Hall. '67.

Fage, J. D. A history of West Africa: an introductory survey. 4th ed. Cambridge University Press. '69.

Fage, J. D. ed. Africa discovers her past. Oxford University Press. '70.

Floyd, Barry. Eastern Nigeria, a geographical review. Praeger. '69.

Forsyth, Frederick. The Biafra story. Penguin. '69.

Gardner, Brian. The African dream. Putnam. '70.

Green, R. H. and Seidman, Ann. Unity or poverty? the economics of pan-Africanism. Penguin. '68.

Hance, W. A. African economic development. rev. ed. Praeger (for the Council on Foreign Relations). '67.

Hance, W. A. Population, migration, and urbanization in Africa. Columbia University Press. '70.

Hatch, J. C. Africa—the rebirth of self-rule. Oxford University Press. '67.

Jeune Afrique, Editorial Staff, eds. Africa 69/70; a reference volume on the African continent. Africana. '69.

Jordan, R. S. Government and power in West Africa. Africana. '69.

Kamarck, A. M. The economics of African development. rev. ed. Praeger. '70.

Kedourie, Elie, ed. Nationalism in Asia and Africa. Meridian/World Publishing Co. '70.

Kenworthy, L. S. Studying Africa in elementary and secondary schools. 3d ed. Teachers College Press, Columbia University. 525 W. 120th St. New York 10027. '70.

King, N. Q. Religions of Africa: a pilgrimage into traditional religions. Harper. '70.

Krapf-Askari, Eva. Yoruba towns and cities. Clarendon Press. '69.

Lefever, E. W. Spear and scepter: army, police, and politics in tropical Africa. Brookings. '70.

Legvold, Robert. Soviet policy in West Africa. Harvard University Press. '70.

Liebenow, J. G. Liberia: the evolution of privilege. Cornell University Press. '69.

Lloyd, P. C. Africa in social change; West African societies in transition. Praeger. '69.

Lusignan, Guy de. French-speaking Africa since independence. Praeger. '69.

Markovitz, I. L. African politics and society: basic issues and problems of government and development. Free Press. '70.

Markovitz, I. L. Léopold Sédar Senghor and the politics of negritude. Atheneum. '69.

Middleton, John, ed. Black Africa: its people and their cultures today. Macmillan. '70.

Moore, C. D. and Dunbar, Ann, eds. Africa yesterday and today. Praeger. '68.

Morgan, W. B. and Pugh, J. C. West Africa. Methuen. '69.

Nielsen, W. A. The great powers and Africa. Praeger (for the Council on Foreign Relations). '69.

Nwankwo, A. A. and Ifejika, S. U. Biafra: the making of a nation. Praeger. '70.

Ocran, A. K. A myth is broken: an account of the Ghana coup d'état of 24th Feb. 1966. Humanities. '69.

Omari, T. P. Kwame Nkrumah: the anatomy of an African dictatorship. Africana. '70.

Omer-Cooper, J. D. The making of modern Africa, v 2: Growth of African civilization. Humanities. '70.

Paden, J. N. and Soja, E. W. The African experience, v 1: Essays. Northwestern University Press. '70.

Patch, Mrs G. W. African crafts survey. World Crafts Council. 29 W. 53d St. New York 10019. '70.

Peel, J. D. Y. Aladura: a religious movement among the Yoruba. Oxford University Press (for International African Institute). '68.

Plessz, N. G. Problems and prospects of economic integration in West Africa. McGill University Press (for Centre for Developing-Area Studies). '68.

Potholm, C. P. Four African political systems. Prentice-Hall. '70.

Prothero, R. M. ed. A geography of Africa: regional essays on fundamental characteristics, issues and problems. Praeger. '69.

Rivkin, Arnold. Nation-building in Africa: problems and prospects; ed. by J. H. Morrow. Rutgers University Press. '70.

*Robson, Peter and Lury, D. A. eds. The economies of Africa. Northwestern University Press. '69.

Rotberg, R. I. and Mazrui, A. A. eds. Protest and power in black Africa. Oxford University Press. '70.

Rutherfoord, Peggy, ed. African voices: an anthology of native African writing. Grosset. '70.

Schwarz, F. A. O. Jr. Nigeria: the tribes, the nation, or the race. M.I.T. Press. '65.

Singh, Manmohan. Regional development banks. Carnegie Endowment for International Peace. 345 E. 46th St. New York 10017. '70.

Standard Bank Group. Economic Department. Annual economic review: Nigeria, June 1970. The Standard Bank, Ltd. 52 Wall St. New York 10005. '70.

Thompson, V. B. Africa and unity: the evolution of pan-Africanism. Humanities. '70.

Thompson, W. S. Ghana's foreign policy, 1957-1966: diplomacy, ideology and the new state. Princeton University Press. '69.

United Nations. Center for Development Planning, Projections and Policies. Department of Economic and Social Affairs. Economic co-operation and integration in Africa: three case studies. United Nations. Sales Section. United Nations Plaza. New York 10017. '69.

*United States. Agency for International Development. U.S. foreign aid in Africa: proposed fiscal year 1971 program. The Agency. Washington, D.C. 20523. '70.

United States. Congress. House of Representatives. Committee on Foreign Affairs. Subcommittee on Africa. The postwar Nigerian situation; hearing, January 27, 1970. 91st Congress, 2d session. Supt. of Docs. Washington, D.C. 20402. '70.

United States. Congress. House of Representatives. Committee on Foreign Affairs. Subcommittee on Africa. Report on Portuguese Guinea and the liberation movement; hearing, February 26, 1970. 91st Congress, 2d session. Supt. of Docs. Washington, D.C. 20402. '70.

United States. Department of State. Africa: this new dialogue. Supt. of Docs. Washington, D.C. 20402. '70.

United States. Department of State. Background notes on the countries of the world. Supt. of Docs. Washington, D.C. 20402.
Republic of Dahomey. Jl. '70; Gabon Republic. Ap. '70; Gambia. My. '64; Republic of Ghana. Ap. '70; Republic of Guinea. Jl. '69; Portuguese Guinea. Ap. '69; Republic of Ivory Coast. My. '70; Republic of Liberia. rev. Mr. '70; Republic of Mali. N. '69; Republic of Nigeria. My. '69; Republic of Senegal. Je. '69; Sierra Leone. D. '69; Upper Volta. Jl. '65.

Uwechue, Raph. Reflections on the Nigerian civil war: facing the future. rev. ed. Africana. '70.

Wallerstein, I. M. Africa: the politics of unity; an analysis of a contemporary social movement. Vintage. '69.

Welch, C. E. Jr. ed. Soldier and state in Africa: a comparative analysis of military intervention and political change. Northwestern University Press. '70.

Whetham, E. H. and Currie, J. I. The economics of African countries. Cambridge University Press. '69.

Whitaker, C. S. Jr. The politics of tradition, continuity and change in northern Nigeria, 1946-1966. Princeton University Press (for the Center of International Studies). '70.

Williams, G. M. Africa for the Africans. Eerdmans. '69.

Wriggins, W. H. The ruler's imperative; strategies for political survival in Asia and Africa. Columbia University Press. '69.

Zolberg, A. R. One-party government in the Ivory Coast. rev. ed. Princeton University Press. '69.

PERIODICALS

Africa Report. 13:49-53. Ja. '68. Talk with Sékou Touré. R. W. Howe.

Africa Report. 13:8-24+. F. '68. Six views of the Nigerian war.

Africa Report. 13:50-1+. F. '68. OCAM [Organisation Commune Africaine et Malgache] comes of age. B. J. Oudes.

Africa Report. 13:52-3. F. '68. From Brazzaville twelve to OCAM [Organisation Commune Africaine et Malgache].

Africa Report. 13:46-54. Je. '68. Dahomey: coup within a coup. René Lemarchand.

Africa Report. 13:55-7. Je. '68. Two Dahomeys. Dov Ronen.

Africa Report. 13:26-30. D. '68. Shifting forces in Sierra Leone. John Cartwright.

Africa Report. 13:31-2. D. '68. Talk with President Zinsou [Dahomey]; interview, by R. W. Howe. E. D. Zinsou.

*Africa Report. 14:8-11. Ja. '69. The changing American view of Africa. P. W. Quigg.

*Africa Report. 14:16-20+. Ja. '69. African economic development: problems and prospects. A. M. Kamarck.

*Africa Report. 14:16-22. Mr./Ap. '69. An era ends in Mali. F. G. Snyder.

Africa Report. 14:23-6+. Mr./Ap. '69. Economics of the coup [Mali]. W. I. Jones.

Africa Report. 14:54-8. Mr./Ap. '69. Moscow's changing view of Africa's revolutionary regimes. Robert Legvold.

Africa Report. 14:8-13. My./Je. '69. Ghana's foreign policy under military rule. W. S. Thompson.

Africa Report. 14:9-10. N. '69. Out of Africa: Yorubas stir.

Africa Report. 14:22-3. N. '69. Dialog: the United States and the Biafran war. R. L. Sklar.

Africa Report. 15:14-15. Ja. '70. Can there be a peace settlement in Nigeria? Kennedy Lindsay.

*Africa Report. 15:16-17. Ja. '70. Nigeria which is not at war. Stanley Meisler.

Africa Report. 15:18-21. Ja. '70. Look at the balance sheet [Nigeria]. S. P. Schatz.

*Africa Report. 15:12-14. F. '70. Foreign powers and the Nigerian war. Walter Schwarz.

Africa Report. 15:28-31. F. '70. The EEC's new deal with Africa; what the Africans wanted, what the Europeans offered, the meaning of the new Yaoundé convention. William Zartman.

Africa Report. 15:10-15. Mr. '70. Ghanaian politics: the elections and after. Emily Card and Barbara Callaway.

Africa Report. 15:18-21. Ap. '70. Ivory Coast: booming economy, political calm. Efrem Sigel.

Africa Report. 15:18-19. My. '70. Amilcar Cabral: a profile [Portuguese Guinea]. D. A. Andelman.

Africa Report. 15:22-3. Je. '70. Dialog: Africa's population problems. A. E. Okorafor.

Africa Report. 15:24-7. Je. '70. Senegal seeks to broaden political base. Robert Mortimer.

Africa Today. 15:21-2. Ap.-My. '68. Dahomey: the end of a military regime. W. A. E. Skurnik.

African Affairs. 67:305-29. O. '68. Sierra Leone politics since independence. Christopher Allen.

African Affairs. 68:245-9. Jl. '69. Nigeria: one or many? David Williams.

African Affairs. 69:27-43. Ja. '70. State enterprise in Nigeria and Ghana: the end of an era? M. E. Blunt.

African Affairs. 69:67-71. Ja '70. Return to Ghana. Dennis Austin.

*African Development (London). p 3. N. '69. Ghana deserves a square deal—European companies share debts guilt [editorial].

*African Development (London). p 10-13. Ja. '70. Africa in the seventies: population, investment.

African Development (London). F. '70 issue. Nigeria.

African Development (London). p 18-20. Mr. '70. Mali where nothing seems to go right.

America. 120:221-5. F. 22, '69. Perspective on Nigeria. George Arthur.

American Political Science Review. 62:70-87. Mr. '68. The structure of political conflict in the new states of tropical Africa. A. R. Zolberg.

Atlantic. 224:25-6+. O. '69. Reports: Nigeria and Biafra. Stanley Meisler.

*Atlas. 16:46-7. D. '68. Tribalism must die . . . an African verdict [Nigeria]. Primila Lewis.

Bulletin of the Atomic Scientists. 25:11-19. N. '69. Africa: a symposium. David Carney; A. A. Mazrui.

Canadian Geographical Journal. 76:34-9. Ja. '68. Gambia: Africa's smallest country. Richard Harrington.

Ceres. 2:28-34. S.-O. '69. Mali: realism, rather than pursuit of chimeras. András Biró.

Christian Century. 86:942. Jl. 16, '69. Tshombe and Mboya.

Christian Science Monitor. p 13. Ag. 10, '68. Senegal erases French symbols. R. W. Howe.

*Christian Science Monitor. p 9. Ap. 19, '69. A decade of unrest: what's the cause of African coups? Frederic Hunter.

*Christian Science Monitor. p 10. Jl. 9, '69. African states grumble over EEC trade pact. John Lambert.

Christian Science Monitor. p 1. Ag. 5, '69. Dakar points up social contrasts. Frederic Hunter.

*Christian Science Monitor. p 9. S. 20, '69. After Nkrumah: Ghana puts the pieces together again. Frederic Hunter.

Christian Science Monitor. p 6. O. 16, '69. Ghana's quest: democracy with a new dimension. Cameron Duodu.

*Christian Science Monitor. p 9. O. 18, '69. "Africanization": high goal or pitfall? Frederic Hunter.

*Christian Science Monitor. p 4. F. 6, '70. Citizens' demands met: Ivory Coast president "listens."

Christian Science Monitor. p 2. F. 7, '70. Aliens are first targets: Ghana launches attack on economic woes. Frederic Hunter.

*Christian Science Monitor. p 4. Je. 4, '70. Diplomatic drums: inter-African contacts quicken in wake of Nigerian civil war.

Christian Science Monitor. p 2. Jl. 6, '70. Liberia clambers for new image. Frederic Hunter.

Christian Science Monitor. p 5. Jl. 10, '70. Liberian integration: detribalization problems mount as minority elite pushes its norms. Frederic Hunter.

Christian Science Monitor. p 11. Jl. 11, '70. Doing better now: Liberia maps plans to boost agriculture. Frederic Hunter.

Christian Science Monitor. p 2. Jl. 24, '70. Republic status sought: Sierra Leone election vote hit. Frederic Hunter.

*Christian Science Monitor. p 5. Jl. 27, '70. Gambia: independent, thriving—in small way.

Christianity & Crisis. 29:150-4. My. 26, '69. Nigeria vs. Biafra: on taking sides. Colin Legum.

Commentary. 45:74-7. Mr. '68. Nkrumah, a post-mortem. Anthony Astrachan.

Commonweal. 90:136. Ap. 18, '69. Nkrumah's gone; Ghana's agony remains. Africanus, pseud.

Commonweal. 91:551-3. F. 20, '70. Burying Biafra. John Horgan.

Contemporary Review (London). 214:81-5. F. '69. Dawning of a new era in African development. W. J. Barnes.

Contemporary Review (London). 215:1-4. Jl. '69. Sekou Toure's Guinea. Andrew Nash.

*Current. 116:47-51. Mr. '70. Problems of reconstruction [Nigeria]. Colin Legum.
    Taken from article entitled "After the Tragedy." London *Observer*. p 47+. January 18, 1970.

Current History. 54:95-101+. F. '68. Ghana: the politics of military withdrawal. C. E. Welch, Jr.

*Current History. 56:257-97+. My. '69. Nations of Africa; symposium.
    Reprinted in this volume: Economic development in Africa today. R. L. West. p 263-8+.

*Current History. 58:135-41+. Mr. '70. Nigeria after Biafra. D. J. Murray.

Daedalus. p 51-69. Winter '68. Students and politics in Ghana. D. J. Finlay.

Daedalus. p 757-92. Summer '68. Nkrumah, charisma, and the coup. D. E. Apter.

Department of State Bulletin. 58:129-33. Ja. 29, '68. Message to Africa; address delivered at Africa Hall, Addis Ababa, Ethiopia, on January 6, 1968. H. H. Humphrey.

Department of State Bulletin. 59:696-702. D. 30, '68. Africa: continent of change; address delivered before the Chicago Council on Foreign Relations at Chicago, Ill., on December 5, 1968. Joseph Palmer, 2d.
  Same. Vital Speeches of the Day. 35:162-6. Ja. 1, '69.
Department of State Bulletin. 62:185-8. F. 16, '70. Relief and rehabilitation in Nigeria; statements by D. D. Newsom, C. C. Ferguson, Jr., January 21, 1970.
Ebony. 24:74-6+. Je. '69. Progress: Africa's untold story. E. B. Thompson.
Ebony. 24:116-18+. Jl. '69. Africa's problems: the other side of the story. E. B. Thompson.
Economic Geography. 45:53-62. Ja. '69. Some problems of regional economic development in West Africa. R. J. H. Church.
Economist (London). 226:35. F. 24, '68. Friends to all except themselves [Guinea].
Economist (London). 227:22. Ap. 27, '68. Sergeants' coup [Sierra Leone].
Economist (London). 228:22+. S. 21, '68. It's one sort of conservatism [Organization of African Unity].
Economist (London). 232:30-1. Ag. 9, '69. Liberia; preserving the American heritage.
Economist (London). 233:17-18. D. 13, '69. A war we could help to stop [Nigeria].
Economist (London). 233:35. D. 13, '69. Nigeria-Biafra: how final an offensive?
Economist (London). 233:37. D. 13, '69. Record breaker [Dahomey].
Economist (London). 234:11-12. Ja. 17, '70. But can he win them back [Nigeria]?
Economist (London). 234:12-13. Ja. 17, '70. The food's available [Biafra].
Economist (London). 234:22+. Ja. 17, '70. Suddenly it was all over—except for the starving [Nigeria].
*Economist (London). 236:30. S. 5, '70. Ghana: one of the few.
Foreign Affairs. 46:584-98. Ap. '68. Man and myth in political Africa. R. W. Howe.
Foreign Affairs. 47:668-80. Jl. '69. Elements of a Nigerian peace. J. C. McKenna.
Harper's Magazine. 240:6. Ja. '70. My summer vacation in Biafra. Herbert Gold.
International Affairs. 44:26-39. Ja. '68. Is there a case for Biafra? K. W. J. Post.
Journal of Developing Areas. 2:211-24. '68. The trauma of independence in French-speaking Africa. V. T. Le Vine.

Journal of Modern African Studies (London). 5:511-20. D. '67.
    Urban problems and economic development in West Africa.
    R. J. H. Church.
Journal of Modern African Studies (London). 7:369-406. O. '69.
    Ghana, the Congo, and the United Nations. Jitendra Mohan.
Look. 33:18-29. Ja. 7, '69. Black America's African heritage. Jack
    Shepherd.
McCall's. 97:68-9+. Ap. '70. Biafra: a people betrayed. Kurt
    Vonnegut, Jr.
Military Review. 49:28-38. N. '69. West Africa: searches for sta-
    bility. J. R. Sadler.
*Le Monde (Paris) Weekly English Selection. p 3. Je. 3, '70. Mali
    after Keita's fall: snail's pace recovery. Pierre Biarnès.
Le Monde (Paris) Weekly English Selection. p 4. S. 16, '70. Por-
    tuguese Guinea: the revolt grinds on. René Lefort.
Nation. 210:98-9. F. 2, '70. Nigeria-Biafra and the UN. Anne
    Tuckerman.
Negro History Bulletin. 32:7-11. D. '69. Biafra and the Nigerian
    civil war. Franklin Parker.
New Commonwealth. 48:29-34+. N. '69. Focus on Sierra Leone.
New Republic. 163:15-16. Ag. 1, '70. The Mobutu style: taming of
    the Congo, Kinshasa. R. W. Howe.
New Statesman. 78:298. S. 5, '69. Ghana returns to parliament.
    John Hatch.
New Statesman. 79:40-3. Ja. 9, '70. Why secession would be disas-
    trous for black Africa [Nigeria]. John Hatch.
New Statesman. 79:65-6. Ja. 16, '70. Who rules Biafra now?
New Statesman. 79:104-5. Ja. 23, '70. Reuniting Nigeria. John
    Hatch.
New York Times. p 51. Ja. 24, '69. Ivorians develop diversity.
*New York Times. p 1+. N. 23, '69. Tribalism tears at nations
    of black Africa. R. W. Apple, Jr.
New York Times. p 12. N. 24, '69. Vital foreign aid drying up in
    black Africa. R. W. Apple, Jr.
*New York Times. p 4. N. 26, '69. Major powers, Soviet and China
    included, find influence in Africa limited. R. W. Apple, Jr.
New York Times. p 32. Ag. 21, '70. Lesson for Ghana—and others
    [editorial].
New York Times. p 3. O. 1, '70. Nigeria, independent a decade,
    shows signs of living up to hopes. William Borders.
*New York Times. p 12. O. 7, '70. Togo, after years of unrest, ex-
    hibits stability and makes gains on poverty. William Borders.
New York Times. p 3. O. 13, '70. 11 French soldiers killed in clash
    with Chad rebels. Henry Giniger.

New York Times. p 3. O. 13, '70. South Africa breaches black nations' united front. Marvine Howe.

New York Times. p 3. O. 14, '70. Criticism of French role in Chad increases in Paris. Henry Giniger.

New York Times. p 13. O. 26, '70. Ghana wants cut in debt payments. A. H. Malcolm.

New York Times. p 19. O. 26, '70. Cars join camels on desert of Mauretania. William Borders.

New York Times. p 8. N. 6, '70. Vorster [South Africa] hints he will establish ties with black African states.

New York Times. p 4. N. 29, '70. Guinea: attack strengthens country's symbolic role. William Borders.

New York Times. p 1+. D. 5, '70. U.N. mission on Guinea says Portuguese led raid. Henry Tanner.

New York Times. p 71+. D. 8, '70. Business in Togo is dominated by women. Brendan Jones.

New York Times. p 1+. D. 9, '70. U.N. Council votes to condemn Lisbon for Guinea invasion. Henry Tanner.

New York Times. p 26. D. 23, '70. U.S. policy and the invasion of Guinea [letter to the editor]. W. J. Foltz and P. M. Whitaker.

New York Times Magazine. p 26-7+. F. 8, '70. How pointless it all seems now [Nigeria]. Anthony Lewis.

*New Yorker. 45:47-8+. O. 4, '69. Letter from Biafra. Renata Adler.

Newsweek. 71:62+. Mr. 18, '68. Price of rhetoric [Guinea]. John Barnes.

Newsweek. 71:62. My. 6, '68. Privates' coup [Sierra Leone]. John Barnes.

Newsweek. 72:48. D. 2, '68. Keita's fall [Mali].

Newsweek. 73:57-8. Ap. 14, '69. Chairman bows out: J. A. Ankrah's offense [Ghana].

Newsweek. 74:44. S. 8, '69. No redeemers need apply [Ghana].

Newsweek. 74:52-3. N. 3, '69. Difficult choice: conflict between tribalism and nationalism. P. R. Webb.

Newsweek. 75:45-6. Ja. 19, '70. No reason to negotiate [Nigeria].

*Newsweek 75:48-50+. Ja. 26, '70. Biafra: end of a lost cause.

Newsweek. 75:51. Ja. 26, '70. The same Jack Gowon—but now he is the boss [Nigeria].

Newsweek. 75:38-9. Mr. 9, '70. Our army is our whole people; excerpts from remarks; ed. by Richard Levine [Portuguese Guinea]. Amilcar Cabral.

*Newsweek. 76:37. Jl. 20, '70. Life in what was "Biafra": an Ibo's view.

*Newsweek. 76:44+. O. 5, '70. Nigeria: the second decade.

Orbis. 11:1233-55. Winter '68. Nonalignment in the third world: the record of Ghana. W. S. Thompson.

*Orbis. 12:984-1003. Winter '69. State-building in tropical Africa. E. W. Lefever.

Political Science Quarterly. 88:337-52. S. '68. Consensus and dissent in Ghana. Jack Goody.

Round Table. 60:27-33. Ja. '70. Ghana's return to democracy. Colin Legum.

Saturday Review. 53:22. Mr. 14, '70. Good news from Nigeria. Norman Cousins.

Senior Scholastic. 96:15-16. F. 2, '70. Biafrans lose their struggle.

Time. 91:36. Mr. 8, '68. Oasis in a desert [Ivory Coast].

Time. 93:32. Ja. 17, '69. Uncle Shad's jubilee [Liberia]. James Wilde.

Time. 94:39. S. 12, '69. Friday's child: Premier Busia [Ghana].

Time. 95:22. Ja. 12, '70. Exodus [Ghana].

Time. 95:18-24. Ja. 26, '70. Secession that failed [Nigeria].

Time. 95:17-18. F. 2, '70. What follows war [Nigeria]. John Blashill.

U.S. News & World Report. 65:38-9. Jl. 22, '68. Famine and slaughter in Africa: the story behind Biafra's war.

U.S. News & World Report. 66:82-4. Je. 16, '69. New country on the rise despite civil war [Nigeria].

U.S. News & World Report. 68:46-7. Ja. 19, '70. Beau Geste war in heart of Africa [Chad].

U.S. News & World Report. 68:26-7. Ja. 26, '70. With war over, a new chance for Nigeria.

U.S. News & World Report. 68:87. My. 11, '70. Whatever happened to the breakaway state of Biafra.

Wall Street Journal. 171:1+. Ap. 1, '68. African optimism: hope seen for Nigeria to fulfill its potential when civil war ends. George Melloan.

Wall Street Journal. 175:1+. Ja. 20, '70. Healing Nigeria: African nation faces huge re-building job amid tribal frictions. Felix Kessler.

Wall Street Journal. 175:18. F. 11, '70. New friends in Nigeria, for Russia. Felix Kessler.

*War/Peace Report. 9:3-5. Mr. '69. Nation building in Africa; interview with Robert K. A. Gardiner. Immanuel Wallerstein.

War/Peace Report. 9:5-7. Mr. '69. A way out of the Biafran tragedy. Colin Legum. [abridged from London Observer]

War/Peace Report. 9:12-14. Mr. '69. Redrawing the map of Africa. J. K. Sale.

*Washington Post. p B 2. My. 5, '68. Bumps in Ivory Coast boom.
    Anthony Astrachan.
*Washington Post. p B 3. Je. 1, '69. Pessimistic thinking may make
    Africa click. Anthony Astrachan.
*Washington Post. p A 20. S. 23, '69. Ghana's army gladly hands
    over reins to the people. Jim Hoagland.
Washington Post. p A 21+. Ja. 18, '70. 4 played in Nigerian
    tragedy. Jim Hoagland.
*Washington Post. p E 1+. Ja. 18, '70. Africa ripe for investment.
    Jim Hoagland.
World Politics. 20:179-93. Ja. '68. Military coups and political de-
    velopment: some lessons from Ghana and Nigeria. Edward
    Feit.
World Today. 25:428-36. O. '69. Ghana's general election. J. A.
    Craig.
World Today. 26:103-9. Mr. '70. Nigeria after the war. Martin
    Dent.
Yale Law Journal. 77:28-69. Mali's socialism and the Soviet legal
    model. J. N. Hazard.